TOMMY MOORE

A Ph.D. in
HAPPINESS
from the GREAT
COMEDIANS

Lessons in Life from:
Jay Leno
Bob Hope
Jerry Lewis
Milton Berle
George Burns
Robin Williams
Billy Crystal
Henny Youngman
Red Skelton
Joan Rivers
Johnny Carson
Don Rickles
Steve Harvey
and many
more...

iUniverse®

iUniverse books may be ordered through booksellers or by contacting:

iUniverse
1663 Liberty Drive
Bloomington, IN 47403
www.iuniverse.com
1-800-Authors (1-800-288-4677)

Because of the dynamic nature of the Internet, any web addresses or links contained in this book may have changed since publication and may no longer be valid. The views expressed in this work are solely those of the author and do not necessarily reflect the views of the publisher, and the publisher hereby disclaims any responsibility for them.

Any people depicted in stock imagery provided by Thinkstock are models, and such images are being used for illustrative purposes only.

Certain stock imagery © Thinkstock.

ISBN: 978-1-4620-1323-4 (sc)
ISBN: 978-1-4620-1322-7 (e)

Library of Congress Control Number: 2011906662

Print information available on the last page.

iUniverse rev. date: 09/04/2015

CONTENTS

ACKNOWLEDGEMENTS

My sincerest thanks, in chronological order:

To my parents, who sacrificed greatly for my life.
To my wonderful wife, Suzanne, who sweetened my life.
To the audiences, who energized my life.
To my "little sister" Lynn, who bolstered my life.

To the God of Abraham, Isaac (which, by the way, means laughter), and Jacob,
Who redirected my life.
To His Son, Jesus, who saved my life.
And to The Holy Spirit, who sometimes enlightens my life.

To my friends: Nick Pawlow, Jim Daly, Chris Rich, Sandy Ehlers, Bill
Kent, Elayne Boosler, Russ Louis, Gus Mocerino, Al Costante, Fran
Capo, Billy Frost, Max Alexander, Jay Black, Theresa Hummel-Krallinger,
Martha Gay, Bobby Burnett, Eddie Davis, and Lee Elliot, who directly
and indirectly prodded me into finishing this book.

And to my long time friend, now editor, John Briggs, who helped me get
this book on paper.

(And to you, for picking it up!)

DEDICATION

This book is dedicated to all the comedians, who brightened my life. This book is as much a love letter to all of you as it is anything else. To paraphrase a story from the Talmud: As Elijah walked through the marketplace, he was asked, "Who here will enter into Heaven's gate?" As he looked through the crowd, he said, "Only those two." He was asked, "What have they done to be worthy of eternal reward?" And Elijah said, "They are comedians. When they see people who are sad or depressed, they tell them jokes and make them laugh."

DISCLAIMER

Before you read this book, be forewarned - I write the way I talk. I write in sentence fragments. Quite often. Really. Don't know why. Maybe for emphasis. Content over form? Maybe because I'm dyslexic and I don't like long sentences. Don't know really. Sorry.

FOREWORD

As a comedian, producer, newspaper columnist, TV reporter, and comedy historian of sorts, I've been so lucky to have worked with and met the greatest comedians of the 20th & 21st Centuries. In my era, they were all household words. They remain American classics. But if, through no fault of your own, you're too young to remember some, I urge you to go to YouTube, or Google them. You'll find a whole new world of laughter at your fingertips.

But this isn't just a book about comedians and what it's like to be one. It's a book about Humor and Happiness, Survival and Overcoming.

We've all been through "the slings and arrows of outrageous fortune." We've all had sadness, anger, worries, frustration and fears.

And that's when people need laughter. Not so much a cynical, bitter, malicious laughter – but a light, playful, "fun" laughter.

Laughter cuts across all boundaries of race, religion, sex, and socio-economic status. It brings people together, it revitalizes, and it rejuvenates. It's not frivolous – it's necessary.

But don't just take my word for it. Listen to some real experts:

"A merry heart doeth good like a medicine" – *The Bible, Proverbs 17:22*

"One joy scatters a hundred fears." –*A Chinese proverb*

"When you're hungry, sing – when you're hurting, laugh!" – *A Jewish proverb*

"Laughter is God's hand on the shoulder of a weary world!" - *Minnie Pearl*

Think back on your own life. I'll bet you fondly remember the people who always made you laugh. I'll bet you're grateful for those people and those times of laughter.

I'll leave you with one quote:

"We all live with the same objective of being happy: our lives are all different, and yet the same." – Anne Frank

I hope you enjoy this book.

CHAPTER ONE

Take this quick test:
My life sucks!
    My job sucks!
     I'm having a rotten day!

If you've ever thought any of these things, or if anything is sucking the joy or the meaning out of your life – consider the following:

It was April 2nd, 1986, and I was a stand-up comedian in an unusual position – lying down!

There I was, in a pool of my own blood. (I know what you're thinking – "Hey, I thought this was a book about Humor and Happiness." Trust me, we'll get there.) I had been hit on the head 8 or 9 times with a pipe (after seven you stop counting). My hands were tied behind my back. A noose was tied around my neck. A gag was in my mouth. (No, that's not the humor part). I was slipping in and out of consciousness. Why? Well, it seems the repairman I let into my house was only a part-time repairman – he was also a part-time mugger! (Something he had left off his résumé.)

Usually, I was standing center stage, telling jokes and doing magic tricks that didn't work, wearing crazy hats and having fun with audience volunteers. They call me "The Professor of Fun™." One newspaper reporter called me "The Comedian who put the Fun back in Funny!" But right now, I wasn't having any fun.

Above me, the man stood with an iron pipe in his hand. The man and I had met briefly; the pipe and parts of my body met many times more (causing me to realize, 186 stitches in my head, a broken arm, a broken nose, a fractured leg, and a couple of broken fingers later, that today was not going to be a good day!).

The man identified himself as a thief. I remember thinking, "It's April 2nd, so this can't be an April Fools' joke." (I really thought that...until the pipe started hitting my head.) And then he said something I'll never forget. As he tied me up and locked me in a basement room, leaving me for dead, he looked down at me and said, "Don't try anything funny!"

How inappropriate. I had been a comedian-magician my whole adult life.

Never tell a comedian not to be funny!

(Also, tying up a magician and locking him in a room isn't a good idea – it just serves as a challenge – ask Houdini!)

We'll get back to how I got myself out of this predicament later. But I did fight my way out, and spent the next six months in head-to-toe bandages. Now, when you're laid up like that, with not much you can do, a lot of thoughts go through your mind. The most persistent thought was that I had to, as the song goes – "Forget Your Troubles and Just Get Happy." It took years, but I was lucky. I had met a lot of great comedians in my life, and they had shown me the way.

Now I'd like to show you.

JAY LENO

And Finding Yourself

"My 5th grade teacher once wrote on my report card – 'If Jay spent as much time studying as he does trying to be a comedian, he'd be a big star.'"

– Jay Leno

It's funny how most of the great lessons I've learned in life, I've learned from funny people. And how most showbiz lessons translate well into real-life lessons.

I met Jay Leno on the sidewalks of South Philly. Nice man. He was shooting some street scenes for his first NBC primetime special – *Jay Leno's Family Comedy Hour*. I was standing on the corner in the crowd wearing one of those goofy hats with the hands that applaud when you pull a string. The director took one look and sent me over to Jay.

With cameras rolling, Jay sees the hat and says, "What's your name?" I said, "Tommy." He says, "Are you married?" I said, "Yes." He says, "Do you have kids?" I said, "No." And with that, Jay looks at my hat, looks at the camera, and says, "God, in His infinite wisdom, ladies and gentlemen, chose not to give this man kids!"

It got a big laugh.

Jay sensed I was a comedian. Any comedian can pick out another comedian in a crowd, funny hat or not. We talked for a moment. He shared some thoughts on comedy. When asked for advice, he said, "Examine your life, figure out what makes you –YOU. Look for the funny stuff, and everything else will come naturally."

Now, you may ask – How do you examine your life? Easy.

One of the first things you learn to do in comedy is find out WHO YOU ARE.

You need to find out what makes you different from all the other comedians out there. Tim Allen is "The Tool Man." Rodney gets "no respect." Roseanne is a "domestic goddess." To find your uniqueness, you make an outline. You look at your experiences, your values, your dreams, your accomplishments, your family, your friends, your habits, your upbringing. You list them all and try to remember them in the smallest detail (a good way to "find yourself" – even if you're not a comic!). And to be happy with yourself, first you've got to find yourself (at least, that's what some psychologists say!).

Your life is like a museum. A museum of memories! People, places, things, and experiences you've collected. Be the curator of that museum – The National Museum of YOU. Walk through it once in awhile. Enjoy the memories. It's all in your mind – and admission is FREE! It's like your own private episode of the TV show *This is Your Life*, anytime you want. Walk through that museum, paying particular attention to the things that made your life fun.

That night, as I walked home from meeting Jay, I thought about my life. And my fifth-grade teacher! She was, in fact, the reason I became a comedian. Her name was Mother Vincent. Most Catholic school nuns had a reputation for being serious. Not Mother Vincent. Brilliant woman. And funny. Always had a joke. People loved being in her class. (Later, pursuing my B.S. in Elementary Ed., a professor would tell me that students retain more when they are taught with humor. I think Mother Vincent knew that Instinctively.) But she went one step further than using humor; she let us use it.

Every day, in her fifth-grade class, she would open the day with a joke session! Each day, three kids were allowed to get up and tell jokes. Nobody was forced to; you just told one if you had one. Well, you can imagine how popular her class was. Kids were dying to go to school. Talk about motivation. Kids couldn't wait to tell jokes, or hear them. Even if there was a dreaded math test first period, the joke session would break all the tension. It put us at ease; we thought more clearly. (It also did another very important thing: it would exorcise the playful little devils in our spirits, so when the time came to be serious, we would be.)

What Mother Vincent knew was the Secret of Kings. When the kings were stressed, or worried, or confused, they brought in the jester. His moments of play and merriment would clear their minds and whisk away their fears, and ready them for the serious job of being kings. Humor can do that.

Sometimes humor can transform a place you don't want to be into a place that's kind of fun. Lying in a hospital bed (after that little incident in Chapter One) was a place I didn't want to be. But for what seemed like 24 hours a day, there was a constant barrage of comedy around me. Most of my friends were comedians! It seemed like every comedian on the East Coast came in to see me. (The guy in the bed next to me should have paid a cover charge.)

Usually an audience lines up to see a comedian. Here, there were comedians lining up to see me – the audience! (I truly realized that old maxim that a man is rich if he has friends). What bothers me is, I was on so many painkillers, I can't remember one joke they told – but I do remember there was always laughter around my bed. And boy, that sound took my mind off a lot of things.

Volumes have been written about the healing power of humor. Hospitals now have humor rooms with books, tapes and laugh-filled videos. SEND IN THE CLOWNS! Why does it work? Endorphins? Neurotransmitters? I'm not a doctor... I never even played one on TV. But I heard once that how happy you are is a direct result of only one thing –

WHAT YOU ARE THINKING ABOUT AT THAT MOMENT!

Think about things that make you happy, and no matter what horror is going on around you, you will be happy. That's how many concentration camp and POW camp survivors made it through their trials.

And so, my friends turned my bedside into a happy place!

I thought for a moment about how I got started in show business. A retired Philadelphia policeman named Emil Bucceroni ran a project called The South Philadelphia Talent Workshop to give kids something to do to keep them out of trouble. I was the comedian on the show. We took our troupe, microphone, speakers and all, to hospitals all over the city. He got the most pride from doing shows in the police and firefighter wards. I remembered what it was like getting smiles from the people in those beds. I guess now, when I was in a hospital bed, it was payback time. All I know is that I was having a laugh a minute! And like magic, my worries and fears disappeared.

Thinking back, I kind of wish I had been in Jay Leno's class. I was a real laugher in grade school. If anyone said anything even remotely funny, I would laugh. Most teachers would say, "Why are you laughing?" I'd say, "Because he made me!" And they'd sternly say, "No one can make you laugh if you don't want to!" And I'd think – "Why would anyone not want to laugh?" That was always a mystery to me.

But why humor works is no mystery. It works because it fills your life with a moment of joy. And it works like magic! You can make it work for you or for someone you know. As Jay Leno said, "Look for the funny stuff!"

Now, you may say – "I'm not funny, I don't know any jokes, I don't remember jokes, I can't tell jokes."

Well, you can read jokes! Buy some joke books. INOFFENSIVE JOKE BOOKS. There's funny stuff there. Put them everywhere: your office, your car, your coffee table, your nightstand, your bathroom. Read one joke an hour, wherever you are. It takes ten seconds, and it will lighten your whole mood for the entire hour.

You can give yourself the Gift of Laughter or give it to someone else – with a book, a CD, a DVD, or even a joke, if you have one.

So here's a joke:

> *A mother goes into her son's room.*
> *"Wake up," she says, "it's time for school!"*
> *"I hate school!" he says, "and everybody there hates me!*
> *The teachers hate me. The kids hate me. Even the janitor*
> *hates me! I don't wanna go to school!"*
> *"You have to go," she says. "You're forty-six years old, and*
> *you're the principal!"*

(Imagine how different things would be if that principal started every class with a joke – maybe even that joke!).

Oh, well. Until schools start teaching the importance of good, light-hearted laughter, let the great comedians be your teachers!

BOB HOPE

The D.O.D. Show and The Meaning Of Life

"Here we are in Vietnam. What a welcome the troops gave me at the airport. They thought I was a replacement!"

– Bob Hope

Some authors beat around the bush. Not me. Here it is – The Meaning of Life. The reason we're all here. The source of our fulfillment. In 25 words or less:

To be known – To be loved – To be served!

That's not the whole meaning, that's just half of it. We'll get to the other half in a minute.

(Do I know how to keep a reader in suspense or what?)

The Meaning of Life hit me while I was sitting in an airport, somewhere in Germany (I say somewhere, because when you're in England, Iceland, Germany, Belgium, Wales, and The Netherlands, for the D.O.D – Department of Defense – doing 45 shows in 49 days, sometimes you forget where you are. Mostly, you're in an airport or on a bus!)

A year before, I was at a posh luncheon for Bob Hope at Caesars Atlantic City. He told me that if I ever got a chance to do troop shows, I should. He said it would be the most rewarding experience of my life. He was right.

So here I was, for the D.O.D. (that's like the USO, but the pay is cheaper) heading up 3 other comedians – Frank Docherty, Ben Kurland, and Rocky Wilson – magician Brian Dean, and singer Ivory Blackwood in *The American Comedy and Variety Show.*

We're having a ball telling jokes and singing songs to these servicepeople. We did shows everywhere: in fields, in mess halls, in movie theaters, even on a tennis court. They couldn't have been a better audience. Sometimes they'd ask where our next show was and then drive behind our bus to our next location – to see the same show all over again! As one captain put it, "We need to laugh sooo much!"

Well, sometimes, when you're far away from home, far from the distractions and interruptions and obligations that make up your life, you get a chance to think and realize what life is really about. I did.

Now, I'm not going to whip any religion on you, but just as a point of reference:

In an airport somewhere in Germany, I started thinking about Mother Vincent. From page one of *The Baltimore Catechism* she made us memorize:

Q. Why did God make me?
A. God made me to know, love, and serve Him.

(That's all God wants, she said: To be known, to be loved, to be served. Made sense.)

From page two she made us memorize:

Q. How did God make me?
A. God made me in His image and likeness.

(That means we are all like God. Wow!).

If we are all like God, then all we could want in life is what God wants:

To Be Known... To Be Loved... To Be Served.

To Be Known made sense. It was as easy as the lyric in the theme song from *Cheers*: "You want to go where everybody knows your name!" That's why Norm felt at home at Cheers – when he walked in, everybody yelled "Norm!" Great feeling. I knew that feeling. When I walked on stage, even in a foreign country, in front of a crowd of people I never met, everybody knew my name – it was on posters and in newspapers all over the base.

To Be Loved made sense. Everybody needs to feel loved. One day, on a bus going from one base to another, comic Rocky Wilson lent me his Walkman to listen to a lyric of The Persuasions a cappella version of *To Be Loved*. When you listen to a song performed a cappella, you really hear the words. And the words to this song are universal. They point out the simplicity of sharing and caring and the wonderful feeling of being loved, and are great lyrics that just about say it all. (They're on a CD called *Chirpin'* – worth getting). They're also in the Eddie Murphy movie *Coming to America*.

I thought, "performers are lucky, we get to feel love en masse." I don't know who the first performer was who said, "Can you feel the love in this room?" but I do know whenever people get together to celebrate life, you can feel that love. Great feeling.

Now, "To Be Served," threw me. Sounded arrogant. What is this need to be served? People aren't servants. That's demeaning. Then I thought about the British TV comedy – *Are You Being Served?* In America, the crazy sales staff of that menswear shop would be more likely to say – "Are You Being Helped?" That made sense. It's just vocabulary. Everybody needs to be helped. We all get by "with a little help from our friends." It's essential. The bus driver, the sound man, the people who routed our show, the folks who put up posters, who wrote about us in *Stars and Stripes*, and who laid out bleacher seats in the field, they all HELPED us put on a show.

So, there it was – To be Known, to be Loved, to be Served (or Helped) – I had just gotten it all. It felt good – but it felt as if there was something missing. Because there was! The other half of The Meaning of Life!

After the show, when I went into the crowd, I discovered that other half.

It was when I shook their hands and got to know them as people. When I broke bread, or usually pizza, with them and got to love them. When I got to hear their "Thank yous" for the laughs they needed "sooo much" and got to realize that I had served them – that's when it all came together. That's when it felt whole.

It's not just –

> To be Known, To be Loved, and To be Served
> – but To Know, To Love, and To Serve, as well.

There it is, folks – The Meaning of Life – all by itself, worth the price of admission!

You can make it as complicated as you want, but it's all in those 20 words.

(Either half feels good. And you can always get the joy of the second half, because you're in charge of doing that. But when both halves come together – Wow! What a feeling!).

Actually, there is a word I left out – People. You see, it's To Know, Love and Serve People, To be Known, Loved and Served by People. So often, we take people for granted, especially in a culture that is so technologically oriented. People need people. And to paraphrase a line in a song from *Funny Girl* – People who know they need people, are the luckiest people in the world.

Bob Hope was right – doing those shows changed my life. And I thank the people in service to their country who made me realize that as long as you know, love, and serve people along the way, your life will have meaning.

Thank You!

JERRY LEWIS
Faith – and No Regrets

"Here's a joke: 'Did you take a bath?'
'Why, is there one missing?'
Horrible joke. Dean and I actually did that joke. And we
made it work. Because we believed in it from the bottom of
our hearts. Sometimes believing makes the difference."

– Jerry Lewis

Believe from the bottom of your heart. Interesting that Jerry Lewis would eventually star in the Broadway revival of *Damn Yankees!*, where the hit song had that catchy chorus – Ya *Gotta Have Heart!*

I have enormous respect for Jerry Lewis. For the people he's made laugh. For the money he's raised. And for the children he's helped.

I was 19 years old and on a date with Sherry Kaplan. We went to see Jerry Lewis at The Valley Forge Music Fair, when it was an in-the-round tent theater. We had two tickets on the aisle.

Sherry Kaplan was tall, blonde, and gorgeous. She had my complete attention – until Jerry Lewis hit the stage. What can I say? This was Jerry Lewis. And I was lucky. I was on the aisle where he made his entrance. The act he did called for lots of exits, always running up the aisle, then back, to continue the show.

On the first exit, above the applause, I cheered, "Terrific!"

He heard it.

I know he did. I said it just as he passed me.

On his second exit, above even louder applause, I cheered again, "Terrific!" just as he passed me.

On his third exit, he slowed a little as he got to my aisle. And I said it again, "Terrific!" But about then, I sensed, out of the corner of my eye, Sherry Kaplan was starting to look at me like I was a little too fanatical. I thought I had better cool it.

So, on his fourth trip up the aisle, with the applause louder than ever, I held back. I didn't say it. God, I wanted to say it.

I once heard "It's not the things you do that you regret – it's the things you don't do!"
I've always regretted not yelling "Terrific!" one more time.

As a kid, I watched the fuzzy image of the *Jerry Lewis Muscular Dystrophy Telethon* on TV. We were in Philadelphia, and it wasn't broadcast there yet, only in New York. But we had a strong antenna, and if you were patient enough, and gave it your complete attention, you could see through the "snow" and hear through the "static." He had my complete attention.

As an adult, it became my duty to give $20 to the telethon every Labor Day. But one year I was just moved to do more. That year, I had quit my day job and plunged headfirst into show business. That year I pledged to give $100.

Now, as anybody in show business will tell you, the first few years are the "salad days." Not a lot of cash around. I was crazy to make that pledge. And when I got hit with a couple of unexpected bills right before Labor Day, I found my bank account empty. Zero. Nothing. Not only didn't I have the hundred to give, I didn't have the eleven dollars I needed for a weekly bus pass to get around the city.

Well, I made a promise. I promised the next hundred dollars that came in, no matter from where, would go to the telethon. But my real dilemma was how to get that eleven I needed so badly.

I decided to go on a treasure hunt in my apartment.

I looked everywhere for money. Nickels, dimes, quarters, even pennies. Turned the whole apartment inside out. Even enlisted my wife. It was fun. We searched everywhere. Under couches, behind pillows, the backs of drawers, the pockets of old coats. When it was all over, we had four coffee cans filled!

And then we counted. I took the pennies and quarters. My wife took the nickels and dimes. I knew I had way over the eleven dollars I needed to make it through the week. We were just counting for the fun of it. Just to see how much we found.

When I put the totals on each can, and added them up, I wanted to count again. I wanted to make sure there was no mistake. It was chilling. To the penny – we had one hundred and eleven dollars.

For the next two days, I told that story to everyone I knew. I was repeating it just so I could believe it myself. I was amazed. My tote board was a bunch of coffee cans, but I knew just how Jerry felt when he hit his goal.

I urge you to start a tradition. Every year, on Labor Day Weekend, have a treasure hunt wherever you are. It's fun. And it's found money! Money you didn't even know you had. And whatever the total is, send it to The MDA Telethon. It'll make you feel good!

A year or so later, I would be on the Celebrity Panel of the Philadelphia site of *The Jerry Lewis Telethon*. Have been many times since. But the year I remember most was the year comedy was really hot. I decided to collar every comic in the city to work for free, raising money for the Telethon. I talked Babe's Nightclub into donating their facilities. I got press in *The Philadelphia Inquirer*, *The Philadelphia Daily News*, and every suburban and local newspaper.

The show was to be the day before Labor Day. Now, normally, that was a horrible idea. The day before Labor Day? Nobody's in town. Everybody's on vacation. Everybody's at the shore. But I had faith.

It was to be tested. The day of the show, there were no reservations. Zero. Nothing. An hour before the show, there were no reservations. Zero. Nothing. I had 15 comedians and no audience at 8:45 – with show time at 9:00!

All the comics – Gene Franz, Will Neri, Jim Daly, Chris Rich, Joe Netherwood, Al Costante, David P. Hardy, David E. Hardy, Doug White, Nick Pawlow, Dave Carr, Ken Lynch, Ben Kurland, Pats & Bob, and I – started wondering if there'd even be a show. It looked bleak.

And all of a sudden, an empty parking lot started to see some cars. And more, and more. And by 9:05 we were bringing in extra chairs. *Field of Dreams* hadn't come out yet, but I would know how that guy felt.

And if a sell-out wasn't enough to remember, after it was over, after the crowd wandered off, one young couple came up to me and said, "We saw the article in the newspaper today. Our daughter has been in the hospital all week. We needed a laugh. Thank you."

I thanked them. They were so sweet. I kept thinking, "What if they had been too embarrassed to say something?" I would never have known.

There's something I have to say now. Maybe it's a few years late, but...

To Jerry Lewis – TERRIFIC!

HARRY ANDERSON, TOTIE FIELDS

And Toys

"You like this suit? It was a surprise gift from my wife! I came home early one day, and it was hanging on the back of a chair. It needed some alterations – but it came with a wallet!"

– Harry Anderson

Before Harry Anderson was Dave on *Dave's World,* or Judge Stone on *Night Court,* he was just plain Harry – "A crook, a cheat, a thief, a liar, and a man I'm proud to call my friend."

That's not a character assassination; that was his official introduction on stage when he did his comedy-magic act.

Thanks to producer Mike Vagnoni, I had a weekly feature on a TV show called *Out On the Town,* and Harry was my guest. From the pockets of that "gift suit," he pulled a wallet that burst into flames; a deck of cards; a hat with a phony rabbit in it; a pair of glasses – with no lenses in them, a gerbil – which he tried to eat; an 8-inch knitting needle – which he put through his arm; and a steel spike – which he tried to drive through my head. Just the normal tricks of the trade, for a comedy magician, that is.

After the taping we got to be friends. I was with him on several nights. I was with him the night John Belushi died. The press hounded him for a comment. (Harry had been on *Saturday Night Live* many times). He didn't really want to deal with the sad news, so he asked me to find him a hiding place 'til they went away.

As he fidgeted with his crazy props he said, "You know why we do this? Why we drag this stuff on stage with us? Because we're grown-up kids who like to play with toys!"

I knew I liked to play with toys. Thought everybody did. And they do.

Right out of college, I spent some time behind the counter of a magic store. Every week I'd see moms and dads, aunts and uncles, even grandparents, come in and buy tricks for their sons and daughters, nieces and nephews, even grandkids. And after awhile, I realized they weren't buying them for their sons and daughters, nieces and nephews, and grandkids. They were buying them for themselves.

Adults love to play with toys. Problem is, adult toys are things like sports cars and powerboats. Those toys come with stress built in. Get a scratch on your car, a dent on your boat, and you're stressed! You'd be better off playing with a yo-yo or a rubber ball. No stress there. It's mystical. You play with a yo-yo long enough, you reach a state of calm that rivals any Zen master.

But you've got to be careful how you play. Play for fun. Forget competition! Competition turns a game into war! Lots of stress there. The stress to win! And remember *Space Invaders?* (Am I showing my age?) Well, that video game might heighten your awareness and sharpen your hand-eye coordination, but it does nothing for your sense of calm. Bad enough trying to beat other kids, but when you've got the salvation of the planet on your shoulders – that's stress!

The wiser members of corporate America know what kind of toys to play with. The executive teddy bear. That hanging row of chrome balls that clack back and forth. That frame full of colored sand that paints a new picture every time you turn it. Ahhhh, serenity! And little kids, under five, know instinctively what kinds of toys to play with. Give a kid under five a really expensive, really complicated, state-of-the-art toy – and, every time – he'll play with the box! The lesson is: Simplify – and we can all learn it from a five year old!

Yes, we all need to play with toys. Carl Jung knew it. So does Steve Martin, when he puts an arrow through his head. Or Gallagher, when he works his egg-beater/lariat. Or Howie Mandel, when he runs around the stage with his ray gun.

Comedienne Totie Fields told a great story about her husband Georgie (who was a comic, too, before he became her manager and musical conductor). She could never give him money to go shopping; he always bought toys.

Once, she gave him money and made him promise to buy three shirts. He came back with two shirts and a popgun. You know, the kind that when you pull the trigger, instead of firing, out pops a piece of cloth that says "BANG!"

Now she's hollering at him. "Why did you get that?" Georgie says, "Because it goes BANG!"

Now, two weeks go by, and he's got it in the trunk of the car. They're driving back from a show in Connecticut. There's a roadblock set up by the police. They're stopping every car and doing a thorough search. There had been a robbery in the area. The police ask Georgie to get out of the car and open the trunk. He does. And there's the gun.

The officer asks, "Why do you have that gun?"

And Georgie says, "Because it goes BANG!"

Simple toys are the most fun. Try something. Next time you're going to take a shower, don't. Take a bath. Better yet, a bubble bath. Lock your bathroom door (that's a very important part) and bring in a rubber duck. I don't care how stressful your day has been, I don't care if you're the highly stressed CEO of a Fortune 500 company, I don't care if real space invaders are landing on the planet; when you chase that duck around the tub, you'll relax!

Some people sit around wishing they were "a kid again." Some will say it was the happiest time in their lives. And who's to say we can't revisit that time again and again?

Adults go to Disney World to revisit that time. Millions do it. Sure, it's juvenile – but sometimes it's important to "rejuvenate." Sometimes it's vital. So don't let anyone tell you that you shouldn't return to your childhood for a moment or two once in awhile. And if the adult concerns of your life have put a padlock on the door marked 'Childlike Joy', say:

I have the key –
A simple toy – and the will to play!

CHARLIE CHAPLIN AND ED WYNN

Two Great Clowns I Never Met and Two Old Men's Smiles I'll Never Forget

"You'll learn that life is still worthwhile, if you just smile!"

– from the song *Smile* by Charlie Chaplin

Chaplin once said that the reason many great clowns stopped being funny when they got old was because, with age, they sought dignity. And dignity is the worst thing a clown can ever seek. Dignity is the antithesis of funny.

I wasn't looking very dignified one day on the cruise ship Spirit of Philadelphia. I was in baggy pants, a floppy hat and horn-rimmed glasses. I was the comic relief in a show called – *You Can Make A Difference*, written by me and three friends, Don Moyer, Lynn Randall and Mark Goldstein. It was geared to show children that anything positive they did with their lives could make a profound difference in the world. And with a circus theme, it also entertained "children of all ages."

One of the bigger kids in the audience that day (he was about 70 years old) tugged on my sleeve, and with a smile from ear to ear he said, "Young man, I have to tell you, you probably are too young to remember him, but you remind me very much of Ed Wynn." I smiled, thanked him, and said I did remember.

I remembered being 5 years old. There was an interview show on WCAU with Ed Wynn as the guest. I knew even then I was going to turn out to be a comedian. And I knew I could learn something from this man.

What Ed Wynn said was, "If you smile at yourself, every morning, in the mirror, and make sure that the first thing you see every day is yourself smiling – it'll be pretty hard to be sad the rest of the day!"

Later, I would need that advice a lot. I was a very depressed kid. Not sad. I had a good life, good parents. Just very pessimistic. I think it was the Cold War. Russia. We had these bomb drills in school. In case the Russians ever sent bombs over, we'd practice survival training by crawling under our desks and covering our heads. There we would be, with our heads under our desks and our backsides sticking straight up in the air. (I think it was called the ostrich position). I remember thinking, "If the bomb does go off, even if my life is saved, I'm gonna have no butt!" I wasn't really worried about dying. The thing I was really worried about was the Russians taking over. They spoke Russian. And that would be just one more subject I'd have to learn! Here I'd be with more schoolwork than ever and no butt! Great!

It's no wonder I carried this impending doom with me most of my childhood. Oh, and it didn't help when Nikita Khrushchev said, "We will bury you!" Thanks so much. When Communism fell a few years ago, even though I'm a rational adult, something in me wanted to send flowers to his grave with a little card that said, "What was that again?"

So I was a pessimistic kid.

You know that test where they take a glass and fill it midway with milk and ask you what you see? If you see a half-full glass – you're an optimist. If you see a half-empty glass – you're a pessimist. I saw a potentially spilled glass, with milk all over the floor, and jagged pieces of glass that I would cut my foot on and wind up in the hospital, get tetanus and die. But I was smart enough not to tell anybody that.

I always had this sense of impending doom.

But the impending doom always seemed to go away when I would smile. I think a smile is the antidote for impending doom. Especially when the impending doom isn't real but the fabrication of a force that seeks to have power over you. (Which is what a lot of impending doom really is.) Oh, and by the way, usually these forces are very, very dignified.

At the first job I ever had, right out of college, there was this VP who took a daily walk through the company. He was very dignified, very well dressed – but he never smiled. His daily walk struck fear in the hearts of all. People tried to avoid eye contact with him; they just tried to look busy. I told my father about this guy. My father said, "Next time he comes through, smile and say 'Hello!'" I did. And the VP didn't respond. I felt really small. I felt doomed. My father said, "Just keep smiling and saying 'Hello' 'til he responds!"

The next day, when I did it, still no response. The next day – a breakthrough – he nodded an acknowledgment. The next day, he said "Hello" back. The next day he smiled and said "Hello" in return. And the next day – he initiated the smile and the "Hello." And the next day, I got a promotion. He told me that I was the only one who had ever continued to treat him as a person – even after a cold reception! He said that people had been treating him like the "boss" for so long, he had almost forgotten that he was a person. My persistence reminded him that he was a person, and that others were people, too. He smiled a lot more after that. And he had a great smile.

I remember a small sign. It said:

I saw a man who didn't have a smile -- so I gave him mine!

What can a smile do for you? Try it yourself.

Look at yourself in the mirror, smiling. A real big smile. You look pretty good, don't you? You look a little younger, too, don't you?

Now close your eyes, but keep the smile on your face. Hold the smile for ten seconds. Now, don't you feel just a little bit better when you're smiling? Amazing, isn't it?

If the Bartlett people are listening, you can quote me here:

A Smile is the world's cheapest face-lift!
A Smile is the world's easiest "spirit" lift!

Try smiling at a person who is feeling sick. Smile 'til they see it. Smile at an infant; watch them respond. You've just made the world a little bit better place.

I found out that a simple smile can make the doom evaporate, but until I did, I spent a lot of time under a cloud of doom. Real doom. Taking-a-walk-in-front-of-a-bus doom.

And one day, on a busy street, when I was contemplating taking such a walk, thinking how much I wanted to die, in the midst of a bustling crowd of pedestrians, an old black man tapped me on the shoulder.

He had a white hat, white mustache, and big white mutton chops.

In a tone that was almost scolding, he said, "Boy, whatcha gonna be when you're old?"

I was startled. I said, "What?"

He said, "Whatcha gonna be when you're old?"

I said, "What do you mean?"

He said, with a smile, "What are you gonna be when you're my age?"

He looked to be almost 80.

I smiled back and said, "I hope I'm still here!"

With that, he smiled a bigger, full-faced smile, with a twinkle in his eye. He tipped his hat, gave me a wave, and with that big, broad smile, disappeared into the crowd.

Just then, I realized what he had forced me to say.

"I hope I'm still here."

I wanted to live.

Some people these days talk about seeing angels.

I don't think I saw an angel. I think I saw the face of God.

But I know I saw a smile.

"You'll learn that life is still worthwhile if you just smile!"

MILTON BERLE

And the World's Easiest Vacation

"Vacations are easy to plan: Your boss tells you when, your wallet tells you where!"

– Milton Berle

I was teaching a course in "Humor as a Life Skill" at Philadelphia's Temple University, and I quoted Milton Berle, who once said, "Laughter is an instant vacation." It's true. When you're laughing, you're not thinking about work. For a minute, you get a mental vacation. Want to give a friend a vacation? Tell him a joke! It's great. No packing, no driving, no reservations, and afterwards, you feel refreshed.

It was at a book signing that I heard Milton Berle admit he loves to work. When he found out I was more than a fan, I was a comic, he shared some thoughts with me. "Every show is a new show. Make it as good as it can be. Pay attention to detail." Milton Berle worked hard at his craft.

I had realized that fact a dozen years earlier, when I saw him in Roy Radin's *Wonderful World of Vaudeville*. It was at The Latin Casino in Cherry Hill, NJ, and I had seats up front and off to the side, so through the whole show I could look into the wings. The show was five great novelty acts, with Milton Berle as star and emcee. And whenever he wasn't on stage, there he was, in the wings, looking, checking, giving light cues, giving sound cues, and making sure everything was all right. Talk about stress! He later said he often felt he didn't always do his best work, because his time was spent concerned with making things right for everyone else on the show.

(I was like that, too. I used to look for any possible problem that could occur, anticipate it, and in doing so, avoid it. That was good, only I spent my whole life seeing problems, or looking for them, or imagining them! Didn't leave a lot of time for pleasant thoughts).

Milton told me a story of how once he was booked to do a roast of a friend at a New York hotel. I think it was the Waldorf. Now, like most, he could have shown up at dinner time, done the job, and that's it. But not Milton. He showed up at 3 in the afternoon and went to the banquet room to make sure all the conditions were perfect for the show. When he got to the room, everything was wrong. He had to change the lighting, fix the sound, even move the seating so that everyone faced the stage! There was superstar Milton Berle dragging chairs and tables across the room, all for the sake of the show.

That night, when he returned in his tux ready to go, he went to the banquet room and found a wedding reception in progress. (That afternoon, the banquet manager had pointed him to the wrong room). He had totally rearranged somebody's wedding! To make amends, he got onstage and did a show! And to this day, there are people who can proudly say "Milton Berle performed at our wedding!"

A man like this has to relax! And he can't always do it with a joke. Joking is his business. Joking is his work. How does he go on a mental vacation?

With a little mental game he calls "List of Tens."

You see, long, long before David Letterman did his "Top Ten List," there was a place called the Friars Club, at which showbiz folks sat around the Round Table and commiserated. And when Milton held court, they always played "List of Tens."

The object of the game was to throw out a topic and then list ten appropriate answers. Like – The Ten Most Beautiful Actresses Who Ever Lived or The Ten Craziest Acts in Show Business. Whatever the topic, it was fun just to rack your brains and remember. (You can read all about it in the book he autographed to me that day – *B.S., I Love You*).

The first time I tried the game it was with – The Ten Best Movies I Ever Saw.

I came up with:
The Greatest Show on Earth (The C.B. DeMille circus epic)
The Jolson Story (Maybe the best show business movie ever)
The Last Angry Man (What a performance Paul Muni put in!)
Meet John Doe (Classic Frank Capra)
The Natural (A mystical baseball film)
Indiana Jones and the Temple of Doom (What action!)
An Affair to Remember (I laughed, I cried)
E.T. (Enough said)
Voices (A little film that came out in the '80s, got weak reviews, went nowhere – but my wife and I love it anyway!)
And – *Always Leave 'Em Laughing* (Which, incidentally, starred Milton Berle).

Anyway, a thousand people can do the Ten Best Movie List, and we'd get a thousand different lists. That's OK. There are no right or wrong answers. It's just the fun of doing the list.

You can do it with any topic: The Ten Best Meals You Ever Had, The Ten Best Vacations You Ever Took, The Ten Best Motown Songs Ever Recorded. You name it! Have a ball! And always add the reasons why you think each item deserves to be on the list; it adds to your appreciation of each one!

I've played the game for years since, alone and with others, and done hundreds of Ten Best Anything Lists before I realized why the game was so calming, so enjoyable. It was all in the words of a somewhat childlike song from *The Sound of Music* –

I simply remember my favorite things,

It's a nice feeling to remember your favorite things. And Milton's game will have you remembering things you haven't thought of in years!

If I had to make a list of my favorite things, one would be the book he autographed to me that day. He wrote:

"To Tommy – a Coming Star!"
Love, Milton Berle

HAL ROACH

"A Good One, Write It Down!"

"In County Cork, Ireland, a prisoner escaped. The local paper offered a reward for his capture, with three pictures of him: one full-face, a left and a right profile. Within hours after the story ran, a fella called the paper. He said, 'I got the guy in the middle – but I'm still lookin' for the other two!
"That was a good one – write it down!"

— Hal Roach

Hal Roach is Ireland's #1 Comedian. As someone who has a page in the Larry Wilde best seller *The More Official Irish Joke Book*, I feel an affinity for the Irish. (My wife is of Irish descent; I'm not, but I just love to tell a good Irish joke once in awhile). I think it's because I have Irish blood running through my veins. You see at birth I was given two complete blood transfusions. And a wonderful Irish nurse was the emergency donor.

Now, a catch phrase is a phrase that comedians (like Rodney and "No Respect!") repeat after every joke. Hal's catch phrase is "That was a good one – write it down!" The theory here is – you should write the good stuff down so you don't forget!

Barbara Ann Kipfer wrote down a lot of good stuff in a book called *14,000 Things To Be Happy About!* It's a great catalogue of good stuff: Ice Cream Sandwiches, Extra-Inning Baseball Games, Bugs Bunny Cartoons, Hawaiian Shirts, Rainbows; they're all in there, with thousands more.

Some people say, so often, what we see written down is the bad stuff. Newspaper headlines. murders, robberies, worse. Every day people do good stuff, too. How come that doesn't get front page? Every day, hundreds of babies are born. That's news. What's newer than a newborn baby? But let a guy die from a shooting – front-page headlines!

Even the weather. Front-page headlines – **"Heat Wave Kills 12,"** **"Ice Storm Cripples City."** When was the last time you saw a front-page headline – **"Yesterday Was Beautiful!"**

TV too! Every day a dozen buildings are being built in any major city. Beautiful, gleaming, sparkling buildings. But let one old warehouse burn down – it's the lead story. If someone gets hurt – even better! There's a saying in broadcast news, "If it bleeds – it leads." There was a great line in an episode of *Murphy Brown* – "There's a reason why newscasters are so attractive. The news is so bad, if they had ugly people delivering it, the suicide rate would go through the roof!" Why is most news bad news?

The bad guy isn't the media. They aren't intentionally trying to depress us.

After all, they usually report good stories, too. And I applaud them for that. Stories of everyday heroes. Stories of people who make a difference. But usually those stories are not the bulk of what makes up the day's news.

Why not? What's the determining factor? I think it's our own morbid curiosity. If we're driving down the street and on one side we see an accident, and on the other we see flowers – which grabs our attention? The accident. It's our morbid curiosity. And you know what curiosity did to the cat!

The media has to grab your attention. And stories of mayhem grab attention. (If you don't believe that, re-read Chapter One!). But, a steady diet of them, or worse, an overdose of them, can ruin your whole outlook on life.

Morbid curiosity is an appetite. Watch what you feed it. And how much.

Whenever I do a seminar, I always tell people to buy two books: *14,000 Things to Be Happy About,* and a blank book. I tell them to read the 14,000 things in spurts, to detox themselves from the negativism and the defeatism caused by bad stuff. Then I tell them to start their own book of good stuff, eventually filling the blank book, and maybe going to a volume two.

But I tell them to make it a little different from Barbara Ann's book. I tell them to personalize it. I tell them to write a "Good Book." A book of one good thing that happens to them every day.

And something good does happen to you every day – if you look hard enough.

Maybe today you took a walk and saw a beautiful girl or a handsome guy. That's good. If you'd walked by a minute sooner, or a minute later, you'd have missed them. Write it down! Maybe you opened a newspaper, saw an ad for a sale, and got a great bargain. That was lucky, that was good. You might have skipped that page and lost out. Write it down! Maybe you got a great parking space, or a warning instead of a ticket! That was good. Write it down!

Once at a corporate seminar I asked for "good" occurrences of the day – a woman said, "Today I was 15 minutes late – but my boss was 20 minutes late!" Write it down!

A guy in the crowd that day gave me the most basic "good" occurrence: "Today, I woke up!"

Write It Down!

You'll be surprised how many GOOD things happen to you every day, once you "wake up" to them. (And write them down.)

And some day, when things are getting you depressed, open the book, read some of the "good things" that happened to you, and realize you've had a pretty great life!

And write that realization down!

My wife's grandmother was a special person. I swear the woman could see the good in anything. I didn't know how she did it. I envied her. I wanted so badly to see the good in everything. Then one day I was told how. Comedian Gene Wilder had a line in the movie *Willie Wonka and the Chocolate Factory*. The line went: "If you want to view paradise, simply look around and view it!"

I knew what that line meant the instant I heard it. The good stuff is all there; you just have to see it. And how do you see it? By looking for it!

Let's go back to the Irish for a minute. That's how we began this chapter. About a week before St. Patrick's Day, when you start to realize that "The Wearing o' the Green" is coming soon ... did you ever notice how much GREEN you start to see?

I took a ride on a bus one day and was amazed. There was the green traffic light, and the green ivy leaves, green in a highway billboard, a green mailbox, a fence painted green. There was green in a dozen different signs. My bank building was even painted green and white. There was green in the dollar bill I paid for bus fare. And green in the transfer I got from the driver. There was GREEN everywhere I looked, and St. Patrick's Day was a week away. That's when I realized this GREEN was there EVERY DAY! And I never really saw it – because I wasn't looking for it.

So, you wanna see the green – look for it everywhere! You wanna see the GOOD – look for it everywhere. If a guy is wearing brown shoes, brown socks, tan pants, a beige raincoat, a white shirt, and a tan tie with little green specks, look for the green and you'll see it! The same goes for GOOD! Find it in people, places, things, thoughts, words, deeds, emotions. Sometimes it will be big, sometimes it will be little – but there's GOOD everywhere! Only look around and see it! And write it down.

But the object isn't only to see the good things. Because along with the two books, I tell people to buy a newspaper, too. Or watch the news. Be aware of the bad that's going on – so you can help correct it!

When an earthquake hit California, people read the story, and millions of people sent aid in any way they could. When a flood hit the South, people saw the story, and millions sent much-needed food and canned goods. When a police officer in Pennsylvania was killed in the line of duty, a comedian named Norm Klar read the story, called a dozen of his comedian friends – we put on a benefit show, and hundreds of people came to contribute to the officer's family fund.

And in each case, and many, many more, the media then took the story of the good work done – and wrote it down!

JACKIE MASON
Look Good, Feel Good, Do Good

"I'm the Greatest Comedian in the World Only Nobody Knows It Yet!"

— Jackie Mason

The above quote was the title of the first Jackie Mason record I ever bought.

We've talked about seeing the good in everything. Now let's talk about seeing the good – in YOU! It's important! Too often, we're dissuaded from looking at the good in ourselves because it seems conceited and self-centered. And if we sit around all day thinking, "Look how wonderful I am!" – it is conceited and self-centered. But to spend five seconds a day saying, "Hey, I'm pretty good!" is different. It's a B-12 shot, an energizer, a much-needed pat on the back. A good thing. Self-esteem is important!

Jackie Mason looked at me as I walked into his dressing room. He knew I was a young, struggling comedian. He said, "That's a nice suit! A suit like this you got from comedy?" He made me feel proud. Yes, I was starting to earn enough to afford a good suit! It was a nice compliment. It made me feel good on two levels: One – I looked good. Two – I was doing well!

Jackie Mason can look at the obvious and see something deeper. His humor cuts right to the heart of a topic and shows it for what it is. His thoughts were the same. I met him many times, first at The Bijou, then at The Downingtown Inn, and later at The Valley Forge Music Fair. He taught me a very important thing – an act sometimes looks as good as the theater it's in.

It's kind of like a painting, he said, "You lean a painting against a wall in a dark hallway, nobody's going to look at it. But you put that same painting on the wall in a museum, with a nice light on it, and a frame around it, you make it look its best – and people will notice it, admire it, respect it." All because you made it look good.

There was an old vaudeville joke:

1st Woman – "Every time I'm down in the dumps, I get a new hat!"
2nd Woman – "Is that where you get those things?"

Being depressed is a time when you don't feel very good about yourself. We've all been there. You don't feel like going to school, or going to work, or even getting dressed. It's kind of like being that painting – just wanting to lean against the wall, in the hallway, in the dark. But a magical thing happens to you when you force yourself to get dressed and look your best – in a nice frame – you start to feel a little better!

It's a magical cycle:

When you Look Good – You Feel Good.
When you Feel Good – You Think Good.
When you Think Good – You Do Good.
And when you Do Good – You Are Good!

So looking good is a good first step. Put yourself in a nice frame. You don't need to be in a suit either! A hundred and fifty years ago, I guess it was easier. It was an agrarian society. You were in overalls all week, working on the farm. Sunday came and you wore your "Sunday-go-to-meeting clothes." You felt like a million bucks. Even a generation ago, the average person wore "work clothes" five days a week – things you got dirty in. On the weekend, you got out of them and put on your best suit and felt "special."

But in today's workplace, suits often are your "work clothes." That might be the last thing you want to wear on your time off! So just wear something that makes you look at yourself and feel "special." Wear a bright red sweater, or a Bugs Bunny tie, or a pair of suspenders with The Three Stooges on them. Or wear a sweatshirt with your favorite saying written on it (maybe something funny that will give readers a laugh). Don't get dressed just to get dressed – get dressed to look good! To cheer yourself up!

Remember the cycle – sometimes the first step to doing good is looking good.

But the interesting thing about the cycle is that it works in reverse, too!

When you Do Good – You Feel Good.
When you Feel Good – You Think Good.
When you Think Good – You Look Good!

Doing Good is sometimes a good first step. Did you ever notice that when you do something good, maybe for somebody else, you start to feel good about yourself? You feel more vital, more important, more accomplished. Next thing you know, you start looking better. You look more confident, more friendly, more in charge. You carry yourself better; even strangers notice it. You might be in the same old clothes, but you look like a million bucks!

Doing something good for somebody – Jackie Mason would call it a Mitzvah. It can be as simple and spontaneous as giving a compliment, or as complicated as doing organized volunteer work. Studies show it will help you feel better about yourself, because subconsciously you know that you're making the world a better place. That's important, and that makes you important!

Doing good for others has a magic about it. I knew this guy named Len. He wore shoes that didn't fit, pants that were baggy, a big orange coat, and a tie that hung below his knees. When he wore those clothes, he felt "special." He was a retired construction worker – and a volunteer clown. He'd go into hospital wards and bring smiles to the sickly. A real mitzvah. He got me hooked on it too, at an early age. He told me a strange thing. He said he had arthritis, but when he "lost himself" in doing good, he never felt any pain. I'd venture to say neither did the patients he made smile.

I remember the first time I did twelve clown shows in one day at a hospital. One on every wing of every floor. To kids and adults. And believe me, adults love a clown just as much as kids. It's a wild thing to see the expression on a serious-looking hospital-administrator type change when they see you. I've actually had 40-year-old pinstripe suiters wave as they passed me in the hall and say, "Hello, Mr. Clown!"

Now, there are a few people who are afraid of clowns. And with good reason. Our current 'culture' has contaminated a wonderful profession with movies, shows, and songs about Killer Clowns, Insane Clowns, Psycho Clowns. Think about it: if you saw shows about Killer Scoutmasters, Insane Scoutmasters, and Psycho Scoutmasters – you wouldn't join the Scouts too quickly either! One day, walking down a hospital hallway, a little boy seemed afraid. His father said, "No, don't worry, these are GOOD Clowns". A few magic tricks later, he was smiling. And 10 minutes later as I walked by the visitors' waiting room, he ran up and asked to take a picture with me. Just remember that there's good and bad in every profession, and that most people strive to be in the "good" group.

(Oh, I've got to tell you this story. Once I was doing a clown show for kids at City Hall. I won't say which city; you'll see why in a minute. Before and after the show I needed a private place to change into and out of my costume. It had to be someplace very private, where the kids couldn't see me. So a policeman takes me into the mayor's office. It seems the mayor was on a trip and wouldn't be using it. As I looked at the austere surroundings, I said to the officer, "Are you sure it's OK for me to be here?" He said, "Are you kidding? We have a Clown in here every day!").

So, back to the hospital. This day, after I had done my twelfth show and was exhausted, a nurse asked me if I'd go into one special boy's room. He had just had surgery and was very afraid of his possibilities for recovery. (They were excellent, but he was afraid). I went in to do my thirteenth "very private show." There he was, with his dad at his bedside – and I knew I had my work cut out for me. He was a TEENAGER! That's trouble! Teenagers think that they're too cool to laugh at a clown.

So I went to work on his father. I made dad the "volunteer" in an impromptu magic act. I put a funny hat on dad, pulled things from his nose, his ears, his mouth. I even had dad screw up a few tricks. The teen was laughing. (Teenagers love to laugh at dads). And when I left, the father thanked me; he said it was so good to see his son laugh. All of a sudden, I wasn't exhausted anymore; I was exhilarated. As I walked out, I caught a glimpse of myself in a mirror, and thought, "I'm a good clown!"

I have so many clown stories. With Brother Knights of Columbus, I clown every year at a Christmas party for special needs kids, and as one of the four co-founders of The Moore Regional Hospital Clowns, along with Ed Renner, Don Griggs, Howard Menke and lots of added recruits each year, we visit 40 to 50 patient rooms a week.

Why do we do it? Here's one story. We're always told by the nurses who not to visit (they may be sleeping). Well, one day, we're walking by a room we were specifically told to avoid. But the woman visitor in the room was waving us in. Well, this was a command performance. As we went in, she said to her husband, "Wake up honey, open your eyes, look at the clowns". With eyes wide open, he watched our little act, but barely smiled. On the way out, his wife couldn't stop thanking us. We said, "You're welcome, but we didn't really do that much." She said, "You don't understand. This is the first time he's opened his eyes in two months!" ... Because you never know.

Groucho Marx once said, "A clown works like an aspirin, only twice as fast!"

Doing good has magic in it!

Now you may not have the time to join the Peace Corps, or go into volunteer work, or even get dressed up as a clown (although I highly advise it). But there are other mitzvahs you can do. Pay someone a compliment, help someone with a package, pick up a piece of litter and find a wastebasket. Make the world a better place. There's a great book called *Random Acts of Kindness*. By all means buy it – it'll give you some great (and easy) ideas. And if you want to be a clown, look in your Yellow Pages or google Clown Supplies and Costumes. Go to the library and find a book on hospital clowning. Then, call a hospital and set up an appointment with the Human Relations person to discuss what you'd like to do.

Do good for others, and the next time you pass a mirror, you'll see good in yourself, even if you're wearing a red nose at the time!

RED SKELTON

One More Clown

"A clown is a warrior against gloom and doom"

- Red Skelton

Red Skelton simply had himself introduced as "One of America's Clowns." In truth, he was, for a generation, America's favorite TV clown. For twenty years, his show was always in the top ten. And in my childhood years, I was glued to the TV set whenever his show was on. I always wished I could have been on TV with Red Skelton. Sometimes wishes come true, but this one was impossible, by the time I became a comedian, Mr. Skelton was no longer on TV. More on that later.

His TV shows were true family fare. His characters: Freddie the Freeloader, The Mean Widdle Kid, Cauliflower McPugg, Sherriff Deadeye, George Appleby could evoke laughs from audiences age five to a hundred-and-five.

He never cursed. But in those pre-cable TV days, no one did. And following that example, I pride myself on doing the same.

Red once told comedian Bob Nelson, "Comedy is like a medicine, and if you curse in your act, you put poison in the medicine."

Now there's "cursing" and there's "naughtiness." Let's make that clear. Naughtiness is impish and mischievous. Cursing is angry and hateful. Red, during rehearsals, could be very naughty. In fact, his rehearsals were always packed with studio crew from other sets, anxious to hear how "naughty" he could get.

But cursing? Never. Cursing is mean and ugly. To curse something is to wish misfortune upon it. That's why it's easy to tell "curse" words from "naughty" words. Cursing? Not for a clown. Remember, "A clown is a warrior against gloom and doom." And so Red chose "blessings over cursing" and signed off each show with, "Good Night – and May God Bless!"

In the early '80s, I wrote this piece for the *Out On The Town Newspaper Christmas Edition*, in homage to Charles Dickens:

It was Christmas Eve, The comic had just come off stage triumphant, and he was having his nightcap at the bar. "Did you hear those laughs?" he asked the bartender. "Bigger than ever!" was the barkeep's reply. "And the applause?", he asked. "You killed, whistles and cheers!", said the bartender. "So why don't I feel happy?", asked the comic.

The barkeep looked puzzled. "Not happy? Why not?" The comic knew why. "Because I didn't make them happy." The bartender didn't understand. "Look at my act," said the comic. "Jokes about hating society, jokes about hating my childhood, jokes about hating my relationships. HATE, HATE, HATE. And F---! Every fifth word is F---! That's such an angry word!"

"But it makes them laugh every time," said the bartender. "But it's a shock laugh, an angry laugh. The sound is the only resemblance it has to something that's supposed to be filled with joy," said the comic.

"The whole world is angry," said the bartender. "Look at the music:, angry lyrics, angry melodies. Remember songs that used to make you feel good when you heard them? Look, don't be so hard on yourself. You're a hit!"

"Sure," said the comic, "that's all that's important. When I was doing heartwarming little jokes, nobody gave a damn. They said, 'You've got to be biting, irreverent, you've got to have that cutting edge.' So now I'm a hit, and I don't feel like a comedian, I feel like the guy in George Orwell's Two Minutes Hate!" "Don't be so hard on yourself," said the barkeep, "it's what sells. It's hip. Have a nice Christmas."

The comic went home, turned on the TV, and just as Ebenezer Scrooge pulled the cover over his head in his four-poster bed, the comic popped in a tape and turned on the VCR. Abbott & Costello, Laurel & Hardy, Chaplin, Fields and more flashed across the screen before the comic fell into a deep sleep.

Startled, he woke with the figure of a man before him. "Who are you?" the comic asked. "I'm the Ghost of Comedy Past," said the figure. "Long past?" asked the comic. "Your past," was the reply.

He pointed to the video screen. "Remember this day?" asked the figure. A hospital room was the scene. It was a Christmas past. And a group of kids and adults stuck in this place for the holidays were laughing at the antics of a clown. "That was me!" said the comic. "Where did you get this?" "You were a fine clown," said the figure. Brushing it off with distaste, "Corny jokes, pantomime, nobody would pay to see that today," said the comic. "They paid with their laughter and applause. Do you remember how you felt that day?" asked the figure. Angered, the comic said, "Wonderful. I felt wonderful. I loved them."

Everything dissolved and a second visitor appeared. "Is there a revolving door on my apartment? Who are you?" The visitor replied, "There's only two of us left, and if we go in chronological order, I'm probably The Ghost of Comedy Present, you dumb F---!" As the visitor pointed to the screen, a line-up of comics about as friendly as a full card on Wrestlmania took the stage. Their gimmicks were all a little different, but their point of view was the same. It could have been said with a bumper sticker – Life is a Bitch and Then You Die! And through it all there wasn't a glimmer of hope, or kindness, or warmth, just the angry pounding of punch lines. "Could they have entertained that hospital crowd? Could they have made them feel better?" asked the visitor. "Could you for that matter?" The screen went black, as did all else.

The third ghost appeared. He was the only one who truly looked like a ghost. "I know," said the comic, "you're The Ghost of Comedy to Come." Without a word, a bony finger pointed to the TV screen. But the picture was black. "The TV must have burned out," said the comic. "The TV didn't burn out – you did!" said the ghost. "You were so intent on using humor to vent your anger that you wound up feeding on anger, and fueling it. And the anger burned you out." The ghost took the comic to a graveyard. Again a bony finger pointed. The comic's own gravestone was there, and on it a eulogy – 'Take my gnashing of teeth, please!' The ghost spoke, "There was no fun in your humor.

The root word of funny is – fun! Your act was just anger and cynicism, sarcasm and bitterness."

"I thought I could be insightful and meaningful," the comic said. "Let the pundits and the satirists do that. You were a comedian. Your job was to bring some joy. You think joy in the face of trouble isn't meaningful?"

"All I wanted to do was make people laugh," cried the comic. "The Romans laughed when the Christians were fed to the lions. The Nazis laughed when the Jews were taken to the showers," said the ghost. "That was laughter triggered by anger and hatred. Is that what you wanted?"

And as the comic cried, he yelled, "I only wanted to make people feel better."

"THEN DO IT!" said three voices.

The comic awoke in a cold sweat. It was all a dream. It was a new day. The sound of joyous church bells was in the air, the song: 'Joy to the World'. The comic flung open the window and asked a passing child, "What day is it?" "Why, it's Christmas", was the answer," don't you know that – or are you just being funny!"

The comic rushed to a closet, and pulled out a trunk he hadn't opened in twenty years. As giddy as a child who found a hidden Christmas present, he reveled in the joys of its contents: a clown nose, a wig, a derby, a cane.

An hour later, noise in the hospital hall angered the nurse. But when she saw a clown, her expression changed. "Get everyone together. There's gonna be a show – and Merry Christmas!" called out the clown.

And with a voice more filled with pride than remorse, he said, "By the way – it might be corny!"

I was thinking of Red Skelton, and myself, when I wrote that piece 30 years ago.

How fitting that on my first social jaunt after that incident in Chapter One, I would go to Caesars Atlantic City to see Red Skelton. In casts, and wearing a wig to cover my head bandages, I was determined to see this great master. And masterful he was. And once again, a funnyman took away my pain.

Red, on stage at Caesars:

As hayseed Klem Kadiddlehopper : *"I got married since you saw me last…it was a military wedding…well, there were guns there, let's put it that way…We got married for better or for worse – she couldn't do any better, I couldn't do any worse… Her brother introduced us to each other…He said, "Would you like to meet my sisters?" I said, "You have sisters?" He said, "Two, Hortense and Lassie"… I said, "Lassie is a dog."…He said, "You should see Hortense".*

As himself: *"I was in the hospital a few years ago, had a little operation. Nothing trivial…Seven doctors removed my wallet…The nurses in these hospitals mean well, but they drive you crazy, "Wake up, wake up, it's time to take your sleeping pill!"… And the doctor, I wasn't too sure about him either. He took his stethoscope and said, "Cough, cough again, now cough real hard --- tell me, how long have you had this cough?"…And they give you these surgical gowns. They ain't made for tall people, boy! … I was cold one night, so I put on this big angora sweater under the surgical gown. Next morning I woke up, they were preparing me for surgery, and somebody was shaving my sweater!"*

It was a concert of punch lines, pratfalls, pantomimes, and spit-takes. And not a curse word in it! I kept thinking how I would have loved to have been on TV with him in the golden days of variety shows. But they were long gone, though Red, now in his '80s, and away from network TV, was still was going strong.

Comedian/author/toastmaster Joey Adams once told me that as a teenager, on his own and trying to break into show business in the 1920s, a rather rough-looking nightclub patron told him, "Kid, always call your mother." The advice giver? Al Capone.

So, one day I called my mother, and the first thing she said to me was, "You were on TV last night with Red Skelton." I said, "Ah, I don't think so. Impossible. Red Skelton isn't on TV anymore. Besides, I think I would have remembered doing that." But she was sure. "It was the educational channel – PBS," she said. So I checked it out. Seems that PBS did a night of comedy. And a short subject with me, *The Road to Comedy*, that I had filmed a year before ran right after a segment on Mr. Skelton. My mom was right, I was on TV with Red Skelton. Sometimes even impossible wishes come true.

GEORGE BURNS
True Wisdom

"I love show business. If they laugh at the jokes, I tell 'em I'm a comedian. If they don't laugh at the jokes, I tell 'em I'm a singer. If they laugh at my singing – I tell 'em I'm a comedian again!"

– George Burns

He entered the room like a gnome. No introduction. No fanfare. The thirty or so people lucky enough to be invited to this party for him were buzzing. Small talk. But when someone saw him milling around she said, "It's him – he's here!" And a round of applause started. Warm, friendly, respectful applause.

I've never been at a private audience with the Pope, but I think this is what it feels like. (Except this was at The Sultan's Suite at Caesars in Atlantic City. I don't think the Pope goes to casinos). Soon he motioned for everyone to gather round and sit. George Burns was about to hold court.

"What shall we talk about?" he asked. And the questions started to fly.

Why do you smoke a cigar?
"I use it for my comedy. I tell a joke. Look at my cigar. It's like a straight man... I buy El Productos, three for a dollar ... You can't get a straight man that cheap."

Do you have a love interest?
"I'm 93. I do it myself. But I wear a glove, so it's safe."

What was the most fun about making Oh God?

"Meeting John Denver. He's a nice boy. If God really were to come back, it would be to someone like John Denver. God would never make the trip for Milton Berle!"

Will you ever retire?

"Retire to what? You know what you do when you retire? You sit around all day and play with your cuticles. Did you ever play with your cuticles? It's boring."

Tell us about your new book "All My Best Friends."

"I tell the truth about people. But I play it safe. I wrote about people like Jolson, Cantor. They're all dead. They can't sue me!"

On and on the questions went – and Burns answered them rapid fire. Sharp as a tack. Trigger mind. Half of us in the room wished that we were as quick and witty now as he was at 93.

Then someone asked a serious question:

Why do you do it? Why do you, a giant star, come down to meet with us, when lesser stars won't give us the time of day?

"I do it because I'm in show business. I love it. I always have. You should always fall in love with what you do. It gives you a reason to get up in the morning. And if you're not in love with what you do, figure out what you love – and start doing it. I loved show business even when I wasn't a success at it. I looked at it this way: I'd rather spend my life being a failure at something I love than a success at something I hate."

The room got very quiet. We had just heard something very profound. But George Burns' face showed a little discomfort. I knew what it was. Comedians like to leave 'em with a laugh.

So when he said, "Let's have another question," I fed him a straight line. I said, "You've been in show business your whole life. What's the best piece of advice you could give someone just going into show business?"

He said, "Don't ever leave your wallet in the dressing room!"

JACK BENNY

An Appreciation of Life

"Hello folks, this is Jack Benny. There will be a slight pause for everyone to say, 'Who cares?'"

– Jack Benny

Later at that George Burns party, Mr. Burns told me something about his lifelong friend, comedian Jack Benny. He said, "Jack would come up and tell me the strangest things. Like one day he rushed over to tell me – quote – 'I just had the greatest glass of water I ever had in my life!' – and that was it."

He said, "From any other comedian that would be a set-up to a story, but from Jack Benny, that was it." Just a wish to share his appreciation of the moment.

That scene lingered with me. What a wonderful thing to be able to savor; to be able to relish such an ordinary thing as a drink of water. How rich you could make your life if you could learn to enjoy everyday things that deeply.

There isn't a comic that's been on stage post-1980 who hasn't said, "Didja ever notice..?" followed by an observational gag. But I thought, along with finding what was funny in a situation, how enriching it would be to use the "Didja ever notice..." formula to realize all the taken-for-granted wonderfulness around us.

I won't give you a ton of them – more fun to think of them on your own – but here are a few things to get you started:

Didja ever notice...
How good it feels to get into bed – to cool, crisp sheets in the summer, or a warm, thick blanket in the winter?
Didja ever notice...
How delicious it is to raid the refrigerator at 2:00 a.m. and make yourself a hero-size sandwich with lunchmeat, and cheese, and mustard and mayo, and a big glass of iced tea?
Didja ever notice...
How amazing it is to look up into a clear, nighttime sky and think of all the stars and moons and planets out there?
Didja ever notice...
How terrific it is to walk by a bakery and catch the aroma of freshly baked bread?
Didja ever notice...
How thrilling it is to put on a radio, or pop in a CD, and hear your favorite kind of music, performed just for you, anytime you want!

SAVOR!

Now, go ahead – start to savor your own stuff. And if you need a guideline, look at what I've done above: Just use your senses – touch, taste, sight, smell, sound.

And then just realize how lucky you truly are to have some of these senses. Some people have them all. Some only have a few. But if you have one or more – realize what a gift each is. Use the gifts. Use them like money.

Just like you would buy what you could buy – if only you had the money... Touch what you can touch, taste what you can taste, see what you can see, smell what you can smell, hear what you can hear – and savor it! Just as it's not much good buying stuff if you can't appreciate it, it's not much good touching, tasting, seeing, smelling, or hearing stuff either – until you start to appreciate it!

As an ex-5th grade teacher, I'm here to tell you, they ought to teach a course in:
"THE APPRECIATION OF LIFE."

People need it badly!

A joke –
A father decides he's going to test his son on subtraction. He says, "If I have three oranges and I take away two ... what's the difference?"
The kid says, "That's what I say – what's the difference?"

Sure, it's a joke, but I can't tell you how many kids look at math or reading, science or art, and say, "What's the difference? Who cares?" What they're really saying is, "Give me something to care about."

What they need is to be given an appreciation of things.

And first, an appreciation of life. An appreciation of life is the real motivator – it should be lesson #1.

What's the use of anything if you don't appreciate it?

As a kid, they tried to push music on me. The notes, the practicing – not for me. I never learned an instrument. I had some ability, but no patience. For a long time, I couldn't care less about music. It was just there – on the radio, OK, but I could take it or leave it.

Then one day in prep school, our logic teacher, Father Knapp (who was upset by the fact that we didn't have a music appreciation course in the curriculum), said, "Today I'm going to use logic period to teach you music appreciation."

We thought – boring!

For the next 40 minutes, he never said a word. He just blasted a dozen kinds of music at us over monster speakers, closed his eyes, and savored – periodically conducting an imaginary orchestra. The whole room vibrated. We could feel the music in our fingertips. We could see the joy on his face.

We could smell it and taste it. After awhile, he motioned permission for us to close our eyes and also pretend to conduct.

He never said a word. But that day, 20 teen-age kids learned real music appreciation. That day we experienced music as we never had before.

But it wasn't 'til I heard the Jack Benny "glass of water" story that I realized you could teach yourself to appreciate anything you wanted to, just by stopping to savor it!

You can do it, too!

Start with a glass of water!

JIMMY DURANTE
Ya Gotta Start Off Each Day With a Song!

"Ya Gotta Start Off Each Day With A Song,
Even When Things Go Wrong.
You'll Feel Better!
You'll Even Look Better!
Leave it to me – You'll be a go-getter!"

– lyrics to a Jimmy Durante song

Someone once said it was hard to describe Jimmy Durante. He was a comedian. He was a singer. He was a songwriter. He was a musician. He was an actor. Now, if you listed the *10 Greatest Comedians of All Time*, Jimmy Durante's name might not be on the list. If you listed the *10 Greatest Singers of All Time* – his name definitely wouldn't be on the list. If you listed the *10 Greatest Songwriters of All Time* – don't expect his name there either. And if you listed the *10 Greatest Actors of All Time* – not there either.

But if you listed the *10 Greatest Entertainers of All Time* – you'd see the name Durante! He was one of the show business greats. He was one of a kind. He had a warmth, a likeability, a command of the stage that very few had.

When Jimmy Durante stood on stage with his prominent proboscis (the nose he referred to as Schnozzola), his bald head, floppy hat, his impish smile and that twinkle in his eye, he could do no wrong. Whether he was telling a joke, pounding out a ragtime tune on the 88's, growling out the lyrics to a funny song, or strutting his stuff in a cakewalk, you just knew you were going to have a good time. And you knew you'd be humming a happy tune all day long.

And a happy tune can be a lifesaver.

I stood onstage at Palumbo's in Philadelphia, after having done a show there, and thought about a lot of things. I thought about all the great Philadelphia comedians I had seen there as a kid: Phil Jaye, Tony Santoro, Fisher & Marks, Ken Barry, The Day Brothers, Yvonne Moray, The DeJohn Sisters, Ned Walsh, Charlie Gaston, Don Hines, Ronnie Sterling, Joe Talbot, Dutch & Dutchy, Tom Cozzi, Tony Vallo, Dave Michaels, Jimmy Grasso, Joe Connor, and other acts like Gennaro & Jane, Bobby Burnette, John Ribbeccci, Nick & Clair Rivelle, Mike Gallo, Skippy Devine, not to mention some out-of-towners like Ben Perri, Pat Cooper, London Lee, Bobbi Baker, and Lou Carey. These were masterful entertainers. Just thinking of their names makes me smile.

I thought about how Tom Snyder had once done a live broadcast from this stage, celebrating the fact that Palumbo's was the oldest, longest-running nightclub in America. I thought about how thrilled I was the first time my parents ever saw me perform there. If you were from Philadelphia and in show business, you hadn't made it until you played Palumbo's. I thought about how I literally kissed the stage before I went on (though I looked around to make sure nobody saw me!). And I thought about the first big star I had ever seen there at the age of nine, almost twenty years prior – Jimmy Durante.

And the reason a nine year old wanted to see Jimmy Durante? Well, earlier that summer I had been very ill with the measles and a very high fever. My parents did everything to cheer me up. Brought me toys, played games, nothing worked. I was in agony. It's hard to say that a nine-year old could want to die, but I wanted to die. And then Jimmy Durante came on TV. He sang a happy song and in minutes my eyes brightened, as did my spirit. I sat up in bed and my fever broke. I wanted to go out and play again (even though I couldn't). And all from a happy song.

Look, if scientists have proven that happy music can make a plant bloom, and angry music can make it die – music must have an effect on humans, too.

And if you don't believe that music can set a mood – think of all the movie soundtracks.

Anyone who scores those things will tell you there's a kind of music for every mood –romantic, happy, depressing, climactic, mysterious ... after all, that's how, as a kid, you knew when the monster was coming out – scary music!

So if music can set your mood, why not keep your mood happy – with happy music! So often, the music we're surrounded by just happens to be "whatever's on." And as someone who's lived through it, from the painful wailings of the '70s to the angst of the '80s, the suicide lyrics of the '90s to the angry lyrics of today, there's some pretty depressing stuff out there. I remember one morning I woke up to my favorite radio station playing "All we are is dust in the wind." Yeah, that made me want to get out of bed! It depressed me on three levels:

#1 It reminded me of my mortality
#2 It made life feel insignificant, and
#3 As I looked around the bedroom, it made me realize I needed to dust!

Luckily, I had a cassette player nearby, so I popped in some Dixieland jazz, and in a half-hour or so, I had detoxed.

It's interesting that some of the happiest lyrics and most cheerful melodies were written during The Great Depression. Songwriters in Tin Pan Alley put pen to paper and decided to lift the country out of its doldrums.

It's interesting that most ethnic music, sometimes from people in poverty and oppression and famine, has a happy quality which celebrates life! A Polish polka, a Jewish hora, an Irish jig. Italians had a plague of tarantulas, and they turned it into a dance – the tarantella!

Do you know that comedy clubs are very selective about the taped music they play before a show? The wrong kind of song can put a whole audience in a funk. Result – no laughs! (There's one comedy club chain that plays *The Curly Shuffle* before every show at every one of its clubs.)

The message is simple – music is a powerful force!

Melodies or lyrics may subtly and pervasively control your mood, but you're in control of the music that fills your life. *So find the kind of music and lyrics that make you glad to be alive.* And surround yourself with it. Start your day with it! "You'll Feel Better – You'll Even Look Better!"

Neither Jimmy Durante nor Palumbo's are around anymore, but when my mind hums the happy songs I heard on that stage – I can't be sad.

ALAN KING
In Control

"Everywhere you go today, something's trying to control you. On the corner there's a sign that says – WALK and – DON'T WALK. Maybe, just once, I'd like to SKIP!"

–Alan King

I met Alan King on *The Jane Whitney Show*. I was with a panel of young comics; Alan was the focus. He was there to promote an upcoming appearance in Atlantic City. He said that "on stage" was the only time he really felt "in control" – and that's why he kept performing. It wasn't even the bulk of what he did anymore. But he kept doing it for a special reason.

In his production company and his other businesses, there was always the need to compromise. But "on stage," no one could tell him what to do – or how to do it. There, he was truly and completely – "in control." He said, "It's a great feeling! Find a place where you're in control."

Certainly, the feeling of being "in control" is a calming force. Conversely, the feeling of being "not in control" is a frustrating force. We've all been there.

Unfortunately, there are a lot of things that are "not in our control." We can't control the weather, or the stock market, or the politicians (even though we vote for them. Have you ever had one break a campaign promise?), or our family, or our friends (even though we may try), and on, and on, and on.

But there are two things we can control – our thoughts and our actions.

OUR THOUGHTS – What goes on between our ears is what we can control most of all. We can choose to think of the best or the worst; we can choose to think of the good or the bad; we can choose to think of the happy or the sad. It is the ultimate freedom of choice, the one that the person in the most oppressive situation still has. And the one that the person in the freest situation can lose, by giving it away. But luckily, they can always get it back, simply by choosing to. You are in control. You need to be in control to be happy, to have peace of mind. Choose to be in control. And choose good thoughts.

OUR ACTIONS – Most often, we can control them, except in situations where we are taking our directions from elsewhere. But one thing's for sure – if we choose good thoughts, good actions will follow almost instinctively.

They did with Alan King. Back on the show, at commercial break, he asked me why we (the young comics) weren't "plugging" where we were appearing that week. I told him that we'd been asked not to. The show was about him, and its purpose was to "plug" his appearance in Atlantic City, not ours.

He said, "Oh, really? Well, we'll see about that!"

When we came back from commercial, as Jane Whitney was ready to ask a question of an audience member, Alan interrupted.

He said, "Jane, before you go on, I want to suggest something to everyone at home. I'm in Atlantic City this weekend. Don't come to see me. I'll be back there a lot. Come see me some other time. This weekend, go to see these young people." (Then he had us announce where each of us would be).

"These people are the future of comedy. And comedy is in good hands." The audience applauded. And everyone felt happy. Alan King was in control.

And we young comedians knew exactly what he meant when he talked about "being in control." We all had "day jobs." To us, comedy was an avocation. We couldn't spend all our time doing it. But the time we spent on stage was golden, because like Alan King, on stage we were "in control."

And strangely, that is the hidden importance of avocations or even hobbies. When we draw, or paint, or do ceramics, or collect – we are in control. We can do whatever we want with the canvas, or the clay, or our collection. It's very calming. It's why, sometimes, in our hobbies, we are the most happy. It's why they can be very therapeutic. They give us back control.

Control – it's an important thing.

As Alan King told his next joke, someone in the control room hit the "Applause" sign. Alan, laughing so hard that his shoulders shook, said, "Don't applaud because the sign says so – applaud because you want to!"

The audience applauded even louder!

STEVE ALLEN AND JOHNNY CARSON
Two Great Comedians and One Great Lesson

Steve Allen as Sports Announcer, *Big Bill Allen* –
"The score for yesterday's game between Harvard and William and Mary is: Harvard 14, William 12... Mary 6."

Johnny Carson as TV Salesman, Art Fern –
"Call in now, friends, don't delay! The number is 555-7777. And if you're calling from Rome, that's VVV – VII VII VII VII"

It makes sense that Steve Allen and Johnny Carson, who shared one great job hosting *The Tonight Show* night after night, would teach me the same lesson – Vary your days!

They probably learned it out of necessity. When you've got to do the same show night after night, year after year, same time, same place – you'd better make it interesting. You'd better make it different!

And so we all stayed up and watched Steve, night after night, because you never knew what you'd see. Would he do some crazy audience prank? Do a wild sketch with Don Knotts or Tom Poston? Read letters to the editor with mock indignation? Go out on the street with a live TV camera? Compose a song at the keyboard – completely ad-libbed? Field questions from the crowd? Cook eggs in a thirteen-foot frying pan?

We stayed up with Johnny for the same reason. Would he do a Tea Time Movie? A Carnac sketch? Maybe Stump the Band? Show some crazy new gadgets from Neiman Marcus? Play with wild animals from the San Diego Zoo? Throw tomahawks with Ed Ames? Toss raw eggs at Dom DeLuise?

Whatever it was, it was always varied.

Steve Allen answering Audience Questions:

> *"Dear Steve,*
> *I was pregnant while I watched your show, now my baby looks like you!"*
> *......Wow! It's a good thing you weren't watching Lassie!"*

When I met Steve Allen, it was in the offices of *AM Philadelphia*. I was there with friends Grover Silcox and Rich Ross. We were there to promote a comedy club appearance; Steve was there to promote a book.

We were waiting to tape that morning's show. And Steve was waiting to tape – everything! His greeting to me was a friendly handshake and "Hi. Nice to meet you. Do you mind if I tape our conversation?" I said OK. And Steve whipped out a pocket tape recorder and hit Record. "I do this all day," he said. "I have a secretary who listens to these little tapes and types them up. Something in them might give me an idea for a book, or a play, or a song." Steve had a reputation for always doing twelve things at once – like writing a book, or a play, or a song. Somebody tells a story that Steve was out with friends for dinner, excused himself to go to the men's room and came back two minutes later, having written three songs!

What I remember most about our conversation (I don't have a tape) was that Steve said people wonder how he accomplished so much. They wonder when he had time to sleep. He said, in fact, he often gets more than 10 hours of sleep a day. But when he's awake, he makes the most of it. Always trying to do something different, never getting in a mental rut. New projects, new challenges, new ideas are what kept him going. "Always try to do something different," he said. It keeps life interesting.

Interestingly enough, he put his "money where his mouth was" – because later, on camera, he gave us a plug (much as had Alan King). He told the home audience, "Go out this weekend and see these young fellows. Comedy clubs are a new phenomenon in this country. A night at a comedy club is something very different – if you haven't done it yet, you should."

(And as I thank Steve, even now, for the plug, I humbly agree. Comedy clubs offer something very different, even today, when they're no longer a new thing. That's because comedy is like music. Just as music can vary from opera to country, from big bands to rap – comedy varies as well. Go to a comedy club and you'll see cheerful comics, angry comics, verbal comics, prop comics, clean comics, X-rated comics, XXX-rated comics, professional comics and amateur comics. It's often potluck, especially in the smaller clubs. And if you're easily offended, be forewarned. You might want to call first to see if the show is rated G/PG/R/ or X. But like a smorgasbord, you may get a little of everything.)

Johnny Carson as Aunt Blabby:

"I'm old – I'm so old I remember when they used Absorbine Senior!"

When I went to see Johnny Carson live doing his nightclub act, I was just a kid. Maybe 19. I expected to see all my favorites – Carnac, Aunt Blabby, Art Fern. Did I get a surprise! I saw a great act in which Johnny did none of those characters. He joked about airlines, and golf, and the toys in the Johnson Smith Catalogue (remember, the one with whoopee cushions and hand-buzzers), and closed with a great "kid's show" sketch – Deputy John.

I was much too shy to try to get backstage. If I could have met him, I would have loved to ask why he didn't do his "tried and true" standards.

Years later, though, he gave the answer in an anecdote. He said he met a teacher once who said she had 30 years of experience teaching 5th grade, and she was teaching it exactly the same way now as when she started. Johnny theorized, "She didn't have 30 years of experience. She had 1 year of experience – 30 times."

The lesson to the teacher – Vary!

It's a good life lesson, too. Boredom is one of the major causes of stress. Do the same thing day after day, week after week, year after year, and it will silently get on your nerves. So we need to vary. Now, unlike Steve and Johnny, we can't always vary our jobs or our hours, but we can vary the little things that can make each day different.

Always have cereal for breakfast? Tomorrow, try a bagel. Always take the same roads to work? One day, try some back streets. Re-arrange your desk. Put a new picture on your wall. Buy a new outfit. Buy a new CD. Read a new book. Try a new hobby. Learn a new skill. Start a new photo album. Learn a new joke. Go out of your way to make a new friend. Plan a party. Call someone you've been out of touch with.

Are you a couch potato? Well, get off your butt. Take a walk. Go to a museum. Go to a zoo. Are you Mr. Exercise? Then get on your butt. Rent a movie. Watch a talk show. Eat cold pizza. See how the other half lives.

I'm not saying replace something you enjoy with something you hate (although, sometimes that's good, it makes you enjoy what you like even more). I'm saying – vary.

Do whatever; just do something different. Oh, and a big tip here: don't ever do anything that takes a lot of time, or money, or risk – at least not at first. Do cheap, easy things. This way, if one doesn't work out, you don't resent trying it.

Now, I don't recommend this. Repeat – I don't recommend this – but one of the greatest things I've ever seen happened in a restaurant. My wife Suzanne and I were having brunch. At the table next to us were three little old ladies, average age 80. We couldn't help but hear them talk, especially when it came time for dessert. One ordered for all three. "Three orders of crème pie," she said. When the orders came, one lady picked up two pies and threw them right in the other two ladies' faces. The whole restaurant looked in amazement. "Now throw this one at me," she said. And they did. She said, "We've been having Sunday brunch like this for thirty years, and I've been dying to do that for twenty of them! The desserts are on me!" Everybody laughed!

I thought, this lady should teach my stress-relief course!

SOUPY SALES

Speaking of Pies

"They say I've gotten hit with well over 20,000 pies in my career. When it comes to TV comedy, I'm a pioneer. Every time I got hit with a pie, some went in my ear!"

— Soupy Sales

In almost 12 years of helping run a comedy club, I've worked with hundreds of comedians. I've never experienced anything like I experienced with Soupy Sales. I've never seen so much giving in my life. He gave above and beyond the call of duty for three days straight. He gave of his time, his talent, his energy, his hospitality – in short – himself! And not just on stage, but all day long.

It started in the hotel lobby where we were to meet *Philadelphia Daily News* reporter Rick Selvin for dinner and an interview. Soupy stepped off the elevator with a big hello and a handshake – and started giving out with the jokes.

"A bishop and a politician die and go to heaven. St. Peter meets them both at the Pearly Gates. He gives the bishop a handshake, and tells the politician they're planning a big parade for him! The politician says, 'He only gets a handshake, and I get a parade?' St. Peter says, 'Hey, we get all the bishops – but you're the first politician we've ever had!'"

About ten jokes later, now settled in the dining room, Soupy gave a two-hour interview. He kept getting interrupted, because everyone, young and old, kept coming to our table and asking for autographs – which Soupy cheerfully gave; asking for photos – which Soupy happily posed for; and paying compliments – for which Soupy graciously gave thanks. When the dinner was over – the check was on him. But he had to get to sleep soon; tomorrow morning would be an early one.

Six a.m. is early for a nightclub comic, but there was Soupy, bright and bubbly, waiting to do a drive-time radio show with me. At the station, he was giving out copies of his joke book *Did You Hear The One About?* On the air he was giving out with more jokes –

"They're treating me great at the comedy club – you should see my dressing room there – it's all tile. With three of everything... three sinks... three toilets..."

And on the way back in the car, when he spotted that *The Delaware County Daily Times* was nice enough to have a big picture of him on the entertainment page announcing his arrival, he asked, "Where is this paper printed?" I said, "About a mile from here." He said, "Let's stop in and say thanks!" Well, the newsroom came to a halt! Within 10 seconds, everyone was crowded around getting autographs from Soupy, who greeted all.

That night's show was a repeat of the same. After three standing ovations, when most others would have said "Thank you and good night," Soupy announced that if the crowd would give him 15 minutes to freshen up – he'd meet anyone who wanted to say hello downstairs in the dining room. The capacity crowd in the showroom became a capacity crowd in the dining room. And Soupy didn't leave 'til the last autograph was signed, the last warm memory was retold and the last picture was taken. It was almost 2 a.m. These people loved him. They didn't act like fans, they acted like family!

The next day at lunch (also his treat), Soupy asked if we could go to a mall and do a little shopping. And every store he went into, he hummed a happy song, told a joke, gave an autograph or two. By now I had to ask – "Soupy, you're always so happy, always humming, don't you ever feel miserable?"

He said, "Sure, I don't feel too great right now, I've got a little cold, I'm tired – but what good would it do walking around miserable? At least this way, I make some people happy."

I've said a lot in my day about finding joy, seeking joy and realizing joy. I guess I took it for granted until then, but that day I realized that sometimes you've got to make joy!

It's important to "Stop and Smell the Flowers," but sometimes you have to:

> Plant Flowers,
> and Water Flowers,
> and Nurture Flowers,
> and Pick Flowers,
> and Give Flowers!

So if you're having trouble finding joy – make some ... with a smile, a joke, a kind deed or a happy song!

And when life throws a pie in your face – laugh!

JIMMIE, MYRON, MOMS AND NIPSEY
Eliminate Hate

"In Ireland, the Protestants hate the Catholics and the Catholics hate the Protestants! Just goes to show, in a country with no Blacks, no Jews and no Hispanics, when people want to hate – they can improvise!"

– Jimmie "J.J." Walker

That is the most insightful joke I've ever heard. (And when the hilarious Jimmie Walker wasn't being a "Dyn-o-mite!" comic-actor on TV, he was and is dynamite in comedy clubs with lines like that).

Let's talk about eliminating hatred, if not from the world, at least from your life. Because hatred is a major stressor!

Have you ever hated something so much that it ruined your whole day? I have.

One time it rained, and my roof leaked. I hated my roof. I actually went outside and shook my fist at my roof. I cursed my roof. I hated my roof. And the next day it rained, and my roof leaked again! Hating it did no good. So I got the roof fixed, and it stopped leaking.

Hating didn't work – fixing did!

One time a neighbor did something that, shall we say, was not so nice. For 48 hours, I hated my neighbor. If I'd had a voodoo doll, you could have made a fortune selling me pins. The next time I saw him, my blood pressure rose. He was going merrily on his way, and I was tortured. Hating him did no good. So I went over, stated my case, he apologized, and we patched things up. I felt good again.

Hating didn't work – fixing did!

Now, hating individual things is torture enough. Hating groups of things is overwhelming. Imagine if one day I decided I hated every roof on earth. I'd never be able to look up again. Or if I decided I hated all my neighbors, I'd never be able to go outside again. And guess whose life it would hurt the most – mine!

Once, on *The Dom Giordano Radio Show,* a caller asked me what I thought of ethnic jokes. I told him that ethnic jokes (like roofs and people) have to be judged individually. Some are wonderful jokes; some are hate jokes.

Now, I've got to tell you, I'm a very ethnic guy. I come from an Italian, Irish, Jewish, Black section of Philadelphia – and I love a good ethnic joke. And there are good ethnic jokes!

You see, there was a time in this country when a whole bunch of great comedians were telling "dialect jokes." And there wasn't a thing wrong with them. Because there wasn't an ounce of hate in them. Danny Thomas did Italian stories, Myron Cohen did Jewish stories, Jimmy Joyce did Irish stories, Slappy White did black stories, and on, and on, and on. And the stories were warm and wonderful, a celebration of culture, with dialects as musical and joyful as the tarantella, the hora, the Irish jig and Dixieland jazz.

They were a tribute to the melting pot of America. So not all "ethnic jokes" are bad.

An example, from Myron Cohen:

So a Martian lands on Broadway. Has a blowout on the tire of his spaceship. He needs a new tire. He sees, right in front of him, in the window of a Jewish deli, a bagel. To him it looks like a tire. So the Martian goes in and asks for a tire. The owner says, "That's not a tire, that's a bagel – you eat it!"
He gives the Martian a taste.

The Martian says, "You know, this would be good with lox and cream cheese!"

A good ethnic joke!

But somewhere along the line, humor got a "cutting edge." And this "cutting edge" (which can be successfully used to satirize) became a forum for hate. And jokes that stopped celebrating people's differences, and started hating them, crept into the catalogue. Hate humor is not the kind of humor I'm talking about in this book.

Hate humor doesn't relieve stress – it creates it!

Hating is almost useless. I say almost, because it serves one purpose. It's a red flag to show us something's wrong that we have to fix, maybe in us! Jimmie Walker's joke points that out.

Now, hating is quick and easy. And fixing takes longer. It takes knowledge, and effort, and willingness, and time, caring and compassion. But when things are fixed, the stress goes away!

The warm and wonderful Moms Mabley once said, "Don't hate anybody, children! There's only two kinds of people in the world, those that are better off than you and those that are worse off. The ones that are better off than you – you should learn from. The ones that are worse off than you – you should help."

Learning and helping – a lot less stressful than hating!

And if years of hating make it difficult for you to change, perhaps this comic poem from comedy's poet laureate Nipsey Russell will give you the solution:

> *"We all are Brothers under the skin,*
> *Of that there is no doubt!*
> *So go back under your stubborn skin –*
> *And send your Brother out!"*

JOAN RIVERS

Judgments/Wrong

"Sometimes you date the wrong people. I dated a football player. He wasn't too bright. We went to a department store. A sign said 'Wet Floor' – He did! ... but you go on from there."

– Joan Rivers

The Jane Whitney Show was also where I met Joan Rivers. Strong lady, Joan. During a tape break, I confided in her about a problem I was having. The agents were making me crazy. They all had their own judgments about what I should and shouldn't do. One would say – do this material; the other would say – do that material. One would say – deliver it this way; the other would say – deliver it that way. I was going nuts! What should I do? I didn't want to do anything wrong.

She said, "Forget it! Just do it!" In other words, when judgments – other people's or even your own – make you uncomfortable, it's time to let go of judgments and just do! Success or failure will be your judge.

Everyone likes to judge; it's as easy as forming a quick opinion. It makes people feel like authorities. Like experts. That's why there are so many Monday morning quarterbacks and backseat drivers. (And some of these people don't ever do much more than voice opinions). The real heroes are the people who get out there and do things! If you spend too much time in judgment, especially pre-judgment, you might emotionally freeze yourself into inactivity or lull yourself into believing that just judging things is action enough.

Better to do something – and then let its success or failure serve as its own judgment. In her words, "You keep what works – you toss what doesn't!" She would show me how later that week.

It's the old Babe Ruth story – he got the most home runs, but he struck out the most too! And it was because he tried hitting every pitch. If he'd spent too much time thinking about every pitch or every pitcher – and tried to second guess – he might have missed a lot of home run chances.

There was Joan Rivers the next evening on stage delivering a hailstorm of one-liners, and amidst roars of laughter, there was one joke – one joke – that didn't get a laugh. After she did it, she paused a second and said, "I thought that one would do well – I was wrong. Oh, well." And the admission got a laugh.

I thought – what freedom – to be able to say in front of 2,000 people, "I was wrong. Oh, well," laugh it off, and go to the next thing.

Think about "wrong" for a minute. Most people hate to admit to being wrong.

Some people will lie rather than admit to being wrong. Some people will blame others rather than admit to being wrong. Families have split up because someone wouldn't admit to being wrong. Best friends have not talked for years because someone wouldn't admit to being wrong. Wars have been fought because nations wouldn't admit to being wrong.

What is the "big deal" about being wrong? Does it come from school and the embarrassment of getting an answer wrong? Does it come from morality and the use of right and wrong to mean good and bad? I don't know. But we all know that it takes a "mighty big person" to admit they're wrong!

I won't get into the story, but I remember the first time I admitted I was wrong – it felt strange – and then it felt great. I felt free! It was as if a lifelong weight had been lifted from my shoulders – the onus of being wrong!

It's fun to admit you're wrong. Really! But how you do it is important.

Don't do it like a martyr – "Oh, I was wrong, I'm the worst person in the world; I've ruined everything!" Don't do it grudgingly, like "OK, I was wrong, are you satisfied now?" Don't do it defensively, like "Fine, I'm wrong – I'm sure *you've* never been wrong!"

Just do it lightly, as Joan did, "I was wrong. Oh, well." It feels great! And people think you're such a fine person for admitting it. Sometimes it feels so good I can't wait to be wrong. (It usually doesn't take long.) Sometimes I even take the blame for others who can't handle being wrong. It's fun.

Allow yourself the freedom to admit you're wrong. Allow others the same freedom. Then forgive yourself, and others, too. All of a sudden, judgments (your own or others') won't be as incapacitating!

PAT PAULSEN
Fear

The campaign poster read:
We Have Nothing To Fear
But Fear Itself ... And The Bogeyman!

– PAT PAULSEN FOR PRESIDENT

And so, in the late '60s, comedian Pat Paulsen ran for president! His detractors said he was totally unqualified, couldn't possibly win, and if he did – he wouldn't be able to serve, and was probably only doing it as a publicity stunt anyway. To which Paulsen courageously replied – "Picky, Picky, Picky!"

But this was America, where anybody could be anything they wanted to, if they wanted it badly enough, even president! In the late '60s, still in high school, all I wanted to be (all I had ever wanted to be) was a comedian. And somehow, Pat Paulsen's real courage for a mock presidential run inspired me.

Now, a poll taken at that time said the two greatest fears people had were: #1 – The fear of speaking in public, and #2 – The fear of dying. (Yes, dying was second!). Now that makes stand-up comedy doubly fearful, because not only must you speak in front of the public, but if you don't get laughs, the comment they make is 'He's dying out there!"

As a teen, I had a fear of public speaking. But I wanted to be a comedian, so my fears, which caused hyperventilating, were things I had to conquer. And I did. Plus, I did it in two weeks, thanks to a high-school teacher named Joe McGill. I went from cutting school, out of fear, every time I had to stand in front of the class, to being an "A" student in public speaking.

Now jump ahead about 20 years. I had been a stand-up comic for about ten years. I had gotten some nice credentials, opened for Chubby Checker, Jay Black and The Americans, The Dovells, (if you were around in the '60s, you know who I'm talking about). And I read that on Presidents' Day, Pat Paulsen was going to be headlining at a local nightclub. I got on the phone and immediately tried to sell myself as the opening act.

No good, said the manager. An opening act had already been booked. A local singer who did funny song parodies. The thinking was that any "talking comic" would die in front of Paulsen. Pat's audience would come to see him and not want to listen to another joke-teller, whereas a comic singer might get their attention and be a complementary opening.

Made sense. I was shot down. But I wanted to open for Pat Paulsen.

So I tried to sell them on a three-act show. Shot down. Not enough budget. Paulsen was costing them a fortune, and rightly so.

There I was, with something that I really wanted to do in my life, and no one would let me. Would I sit home that night, lick my wounds and wait 'til the performance passed? No!

That afternoon I showed up at the club. The owner didn't know me from Adam and didn't care to. I approached him personally. I wanted to be on that show!

He shot down my opening act offer – already had one. He shot down my three-man show offer – no budget. He even shot down my offer to work for free – talk about humiliating. But I didn't give up.

I looked him straight in the eye and said, "You know, if I do an extra 15 minutes upfront, for free, you'll probably have time to sell an extra round of drinks to the crowd!" I was booked! As I left his office he asked, "What do you get out of this?" What I wanted to say was – the kick of opening for a hero. What I replied was a little smarter. I said, "You watch me. If you like me, consider me for future work." I knew this was almost nonsense, in that he never had a comedian in this club before and wasn't planning to have another. The Pat Paulsen date was a Presidents' Day novelty; he didn't even know if it would work. His crowd was used to music – not comedians!

So here it was:

A club that had never had a comedian before.

A crowd that didn't want to see me.

An owner who didn't even want me for free!

And the consensus of opinion that any comic who tried to open for Pat Paulsen would die!

Add to that the fact that by the next day every comic in town would know I'd talked myself onto the show, so if I died, it would add insult to injury.

But I wanted to be on that show.

As I was introduced, I could feel myself hyperventilating for the first time in 20 years. I dug in and went to work! For 15 glorious minutes the laughs came fast and furious.

The crowd cheered.

And as I walked offstage, the owner pulled me aside, told me he decided half-way through my act to have a regular comedy night, and said "Name your price – If you can put some comedy shows together, I'll book you for 12 weeks!"

As if that wasn't excitement enough, when I walked by the bar where Pat Paulsen sat waiting to go on, the star yelled across the bar, "Great delivery!"

I thought later, was I ever afraid of "dying?" No. I was only afraid of someday saying I had never been on stage with Pat Paulsen. If there's something you want to do in life, you've got to do it.

That night I went home and played a Pat Paulsen album I had. On it was a strange song written by Allan Sherman. It was called *Have I Ever Really Lived?* Almost every word in the lyrics was a one-syllable word. The song was that simple.

It was filled with words that represented milestones in a person's life. Words like: *Born ... crawl ... stand ... fall ... play ... grow ... learn ... know.* And as a life is chronicled by all those achievements, a chilling fear sets in as death comes near. The fear that in the everyday business of living, a few important things were never even tried.

The lyrics to *Have I Ever Really Lived?* are so poignant you soon forget that its singer – Pat Paulsen – isn't really a singer at all. (But he pulls it off – it's a matter of delivery.)

And when I heard those lyrics, I realized that most people aren't afraid of dying – they're afraid of never having lived.

If there's something you want to do in life – even running for president – do it, and forget your fears.

RICHARD PRYOR, STEVE MARTIN, ELAYNE BOOSLER AND IRWIN COREY

The Little Voice

"Remember, wherever you go – there you are! ...And if we don't change direction soon, we'll wind up where we're going...but most importantly, remember, a man's good name is his gold...You know who said that? Morris Gold."

– Professor Irwin Corey

Now, the advice in this chapter may seem to contradict the advice previously given to "go after something you REALLY want, no matter what," but it doesn't. It compliments it. Because what it says is, "If there's something you DON'T really want, know when to say NO!"

It was to be a very special night at the Improv in New York. It was the early '70s. It was 'Open Stage Night.' And tonight was special because, sitting at opposite ends of the room, both in white suits, both obviously ready to perform, were Richard Pryor and Steve Martin.

Elayne Boosler was the host. I was in the audience. A spectator. I think it was the last time I ever paid to get into a comedy club. My full-of-my-self self had been a Philly comic for a couple of years. I'd decided to take the train to New York, or rather Mecca, The Improv, to see how they did it up there. I was arrogantly sure I was "ready" for New York. (Do you remember being 21?)

Then Elayne Boosler took the stage. In a 10-minute set that was so tight, so polished, such a tour de force of comedy, she had the audience in the palm of here hand. Every word, every inflection, every move was perfect. The 'little voice' inside me said, "Time to go back to the drawing board – maybe for a couple of years."

After her dynamite set, she said "We have a very special guest lecturer tonight, he is The Word's Foremost Authority – Professor Irwin Corey!" As the music played a college commencement rendition of *Pomp & Circumstance*, Irwin Corey took the stage to give a valedictory address of sorts. In baggy pants, a British tailcoat, black and white sneakers, a shoestring bow tie that hung below his knees, and pre-punk hair that jutted out from every angle, he was the perfect absent-minded professor.

For three whole minutes he said – NOTHING! And he had the audience in complete hysterics. He would walk to the microphone, look unprepared, and back away. He would compose himself, then do it again. And again. He would walk up and look undecided. Back away. And do it again. And again. It was something Chaplinesque, artistic. He then reached into his breast pocket and pulled out a pack of index cards. He'd review his notes. Put them away. Approach the microphone, then back off, and review them again. By now the audience was howling! And he hadn't said a word. On his third attempt at reviewing the notes, he'd fumble & drop all the cards. The next sixty seconds was spent picking them up and putting them back in the right order. Over and over again. And finally, as the crowd was gasping for breath from laughter, he had a confident look on his face. The cards were in perfect order! He approached the microphone, and reading from the first card, he spoke his first word – "However!" The crowd roared! (His characteristic bumbling hid the fact that he is, even at age ninety, an astute, well-informed, brilliant man.)

For the next two hours (yes, I said two hours) he tore the crowd apart. It was now time for all the other comics to take their turn. As we looked around, Richard Pryor and Steve Martin were - GONE! That finely tuned sense of right and wrong that we sometimes call "the little voice inside us" told them that to take the stage now would be futile. Irwin Corey had wrung the crowd dry.

Others, whose senses weren't so finely tuned, gave it a shot. With great material, they sweated it out, and faced a crowd that looked back almost apologetically saying, "Sorry, you're funny – but we don't have a laugh left in us."

Coincidentally, a dozen years later, Elayne Boosler would do a deodorant commercial, the copy of which read, "In comedy, never follow a comedian who's better than you. And never let 'em see you sweat!"

And so, Steve Martin and Richard Pryor listened to that 'little voice." So did I. Remembering Elayne's set, I went back to Philadelphia and the drawing board.

We've all been there, when that 'little voice' inside you says, "Uh-uh." And we know it's real. Because we know the 'little voice' isn't guided by fear, but by strength. The strength of better judgment. The strength of an informed opinion. It's the same advice Kenny Rogers gave in the song *The Gambler* – " know when to hold 'em…know when to fold 'em." And when you follow the advice of that 'little voice,' the one that says, "Don't go down that street. Turn around, walk away," you never regret it.

You never regret it because, when all your friends say, "Go ahead, do it," when blind ambition says, "Jump in," your wisest friend (that 'little voice' inside you that usually says "Try harder") is saying," No thank you!" And it's saying it with great assuredness.

It's the same assuredness with which it says, "If you REALLY want something – Go for it." (And P.S. – You never have to consult that 'little voice.' It always volunteers, like the kid in school wildly waving his hand at the teacher because he KNOWS the answer.)

Listen to that 'little voice'. It's a wise friend.

JOEY BISHOP

The Risk of Being Yourself

"So Sam is a good man, just not handsome. But he always wanted to be handsome. One day he hits the lottery, takes the money and goes wild. He gets a nose job, a face-lift, a hair transplant, his teeth capped. He gets liposuction and loses a hundred pounds. He's gorgeous. The next day he gets hit by a bus and drops dead. He goes to heaven and sees God. He says 'God, I was always a good man, why did you let this happen?' God says, 'Sam – I'm sorry! I didn't recognize you!'"

– Joey Bishop

Joey Bishop was one of the quickest minds in comedy. That's not just my opinion; dozens of superstars say the same. And his formula was a simple one – forget about pretense. Be honest; be yourself; take what you've got and work with it.

Once he worked a nightclub with a very small audience, and said – "I like a small crowd. This way if I don't do good – not too many people know about it!" He diffused all the anxiety. He just came out, was honest, was himself, and went with it.

Sometimes that's the toughest thing to do. But once, Joey claims, an old Italian man gave him the best advice he ever got – in just five words of broken English. The old Italian man said – "You do whatta you be!"

Now Shakespeare might have expressed it more eloquently when he said, "To thine own self be true," but it took him an extra word!

I identified more closely with Joey Bishop than with Shakespeare. Like me, he was from a neighborhood in Philadelphia. (If I had been from Shakespeare's neighborhood, I would have said "as was I" in the previous sentence.) You see, I was a straight-A student in grade school, got a 3.25 in college, but I didn't graduate high school – because of Joey Bishop. I did, however, survive high school, and maybe life, because of him!

Let me explain:

What happened was, as a straight-A'er, I found myself in a very aristocratic prep school. Main Line, highbrow, crest-on-the-pocket stuff. Way out of my economic and social league.

Now, I was a bright kid, but I was from "the neighborhood," and my language was peppered with "dees, dems, and dose." I knew I wouldn't fit in. So for three-and-a-half years I tried to be what I wasn't – and for three-and-a-half years I fell flat on my face.

I had two sanctuaries – one was the refrigerator, the other the TV. The fridge was full of food – and *The Joey Bishop Show* (a late-night talk show) was on TV 'til 1 a.m. Soon I weighed 300 pounds and was falling asleep in class! The weight got me out of gym class; the lack of sleep got me bad marks in all my other classes. But it was worth every groggy minute. I learned the most important lesson of my life not in high school, but from *The Joey Bishop Show.*

God, I loved *The Joey Bishop Show.* I think if I'd had to choose between the two, I'd have given up food for it. Joey used to showcase all the comics who didn't fit into the mold of the other network shows. He brought on friends like Gene Baylos, Jackie Miles, Herky Styles, Paul Gilbert, Buddy Lewis, Simmy Bow, Sammy Shore, Lou Alexander, Mickey Marvin, and so many more. And he was smart enough to let them do what was uniquely theirs. "You do whatta you be!"

Joey explained his personal philosophy this way: Once, a young singer named Robin Wilson was booked to do his show. She told him she was used to singing barefoot. It was how she felt most comfortable. She asked his advice. Should she go on network TV, coast to coast, barefoot?

He told her – YES! Because if you do things the way you want to do them, you run only one risk – that the people won't like you! But if you do things the way you think they want you to do them, you run two risks – # 1 – They still won't like you, and you'll always wonder if it would have been better to do it your way, and #2 – That they will like you, and you'll be stuck doing it their way forever, just to please them!

(How many of us have been so desperate to be loved that we changed ourselves, only to realize that the one we made them love wasn't the real us?)

I hadn't even been that lucky. In high school, the guy I changed myself into was still pretty unpopular. So I decided after three-and-a-half years to be myself. I started telling jokes with "dees, dems, and dose" – and people started liking me! Every time I opened my mouth, I had a crowd around me. I had new friends. In the last six months, I was popular. (My grades picked up, too, but not enough to graduate.)

Three months later, though, I had my diploma, and was accepted into college!

And three months later, I lost 110 pounds (which I never gained back).

Vegetables and fruit was the diet -- self-esteem was the maintenance.

And I was myself again! Thanks to Joey Bishop!

DAVID BRENNER

Thank You!

Walking on to thunderous applause, acknowledging the crowd: "Thank you. Thank you. Thank you very much... I recognize you... Are you from my old neighborhood? Did you steal my bike? I had to ride the 31 bus because of you!"

– David Brenner

I don't know why it amazes me that David Brenner rode through Philadelphia on the 31 bus. (I know why it amazes me. The 31 bus went right past my house. And I never knew he was on it.)

Every time I've seen David Brenner perform, the applause was overwhelming. It always took several "Thank yous" to calm the audience down. They were heartfelt thank yous, deep and warm. Well, one night after his show in Atlantic City, I was waiting in line to see him, along with a lot of other well-wishers. And a representative of the casino came out and said, "Mr. Brenner is very tired and won't be seeing anyone, thank you." Then she tapped me on the shoulder and said, "Except you."

Wow, did I feel important!

Now it's not that David and I know each other. It was just that I had done a newspaper review of his only ever comedy record, *Excuse Me, Are You Reading That Paper?* and he wanted to say "Thank you." There I was in his dressing room, and you want to talk about busy! He had agents, managers, phones ringing, deals being set up – he had just released the album, written a book and started a late-night talk show – but he found time to personally say "Thank you."

Talking with him for a few minutes, he was sounding out a bit, remembering when he was a highly paid documentary producer at KYW-TV before his comedy career. He said he never understood it. He would be in elevators, in lobbies of these big office buildings, and all these high-paid management types in $500 suits always looked grim – and in would walk a delivery guy (making tops $3.00 an hour) and this guy would be whistling and happy. Why? Maybe it was lack of stress. But I didn't think so. Oh well, another of life's questions left unanswered. Soon we said our "good-byes," but I thought about it all night!

You see, I had been in both situations. I had been in lower management (OK, I only wore $99 suits), and a year before I had been a $3.00-an-hour courier for the same company. And David was right. I was much happier as a courier.

Why?

It took me all night to figure it out. It was the "Thank yous!" I never got many "Thank yous" in management. Oh, I got evaluations and raises, but very few "Thank yous." The day-to-day things I did were just taken for granted. I never felt important.

Now, as a courier – Wow! I got "Thank yous" all the time. And heartfelt ones! Sometimes I'd bring in one package and get three "Thank yous" – one from the person sending it, one from the person receiving it, and upon returning, another from the person I reported the delivery to. These people were really glad to see me. Their urgent, hand-delivered correspondence was very important, and their appreciation made me feel important every hour of every day, even on bad days.

I've got to tell you this 9-to-5 story (actually, a 9-to-5:07 story).

The worst day of my life (pre-Chapter One) was spent as a courier. I had in my hand a very important package. A multi-million-dollar contract would be awarded upon its timely arrival. If it did not arrive on time – better not to think about it.

It was a Friday. I had to go from suburban Philadelphia to the Department of the Army in Washington, D.C. The package had to be there by 5 p.m. – and the receipt had to be stamped with the time of arrival. Millions of dollars rested on this.

No expense was to be spared. I had to get receipts for it all: a train into Philadelphia, a Metro liner to D.C., a cab to the Department of the Army, and the same for my return. I could even have lunch on the train; the company would pick up the tab. I was even to make a collect call from Washington back to the home office to let them know that the package had been delivered – and at what time.

The package was ready late – 12:45. When I picked it up they said "Thank you" with a look that said, "A lot is riding on this!" I hopped on the train, got to Philly by 1:25 – just in time to catch a 1:30 Metro liner – it was tight, but from now on it was a piece of cake. An easy day! Then it happened. Somewhere outside Baltimore, the Metro liner broke down. There we sat, fifteen minutes, a half-hour, longer and longer. I was getting more and more nervous. Talk about stress. My stomach was too nervous to even let me think about eating lunch. I was twenty-one years old and I could feel my hair turning gray.

Once the train regained power, I went to the phone on board (which had been out, as well), and at something like $9 a minute, called the office to tell them of my dilemma. I suggested that if they could get a duplicate package and a guy in a fast car, they might want to send a back-up. No good. This package was one of a kind. They told me to do the best I could, and they said "Thank you."

The train pulled into D.C. at 4:45 – and I ran through the station into pouring rain. Get a cab? At 4:45 on Friday? In the rain? Right! But I was determined. With no umbrella, I stood in the street waving cash! I got a cab. When we reached the Department of the Army, I knew I was sunk as hordes of people were filing out of the buildings. It was 5:01 by my watch. The rain had stopped, but I was soaked to the skin clutching my little package. I told the guard the Cliff's Notes version of my tense story, and I must have looked so pathetic that he showed me a short cut to the sergeant's office.

I ran down what seemed like a maze of green hallways, and when I arrived, winded, I caught a break – someone was still there. But it wasn't the sergeant. It was a clerk. He told me the sergeant had left at noon. I gave him the long, more pathetic version of my story, and how the package had to be there by 5 o'clock – or else. We both looked at the clock above him, it was 5:07. He said, "Let's see what I can do." In a minute, he returned saying, "All I can do is take your package – and stamp your receipt." I said, "Thank you." On the way out, the guard asked, "Did you make it?" I said, "No, but thank you for trying to help."

Back at the train station, I called the office and told them I didn't make it. They said, "Thanks for trying." Talk about dejected. All the way home on the train I just kept thinking about how I let everybody down. When I arrived in Philly, I was still soaking wet.

Waiting outside on the platform for a train home, I was near tears. I was wet and tired from the tension; I had let everybody down; I definitely would catch a cold from the rain; probably would lose my job on Monday; and I had a whole weekend to think about it! I thought to myself "Things couldn't get worse!"

And just then, a bird made a deposit on my head!

I was 21 years old. In my 21 years of life, a bird had never done that before. This particular bird took this very moment in time, and this special aim, to give me a first in my life.

When I realized what had happened – I laughed. I laughed hard and out loud. I actually thanked the bird as he flew away. He had made me laugh! He had broken the tension. He had given me back the weekend to enjoy.

I spent most of the weekend telling the story – as a comedy of errors – with the bird as a punch line, and I laughed a lot. But Monday came quickly.

I went into work thinking – "How can I face these people with $67 dollars' worth of receipts for cabs and railroad tickets when I had lost them millions?" I told them the whole long story. The serious version. Told them I'd pay for everything. They said, "Thank you, but it's OK."

I gave them the expense receipts and the time-stamped Army receipt for the package.

They gave me a voucher for the $67. As I walked out (surprisingly not fired), the company vice president read the Army's receipt. He asked, "Son, what time did you say you delivered this?" I replied, "5:07." He said, "Somebody must really like you – they stamped it 16:07 – that's 4:07 military time!"

As I went to the cashier's office, I thought about laughter, and I was glad I had laughed the weekend away. And I thought about the guard, and the clerk, and the bird – and I was glad I said the thank yous.

Thank yous are important. They make people feel good, especially when they're said with warmth and feeling. They make people feel acknowledged, important. People need that. So, that being said – here's another story David Brenner loves to tell:

"It was the day after my first ever appearance on The Tonight Show. I was riding the subway, and a rather strange-looking lady points to me and says, 'Ooooh, you're funny!' I figure she saw me on the show. So I got up and said, 'Thank you very much!'... And then she proceeded, one by one, to point to every single person on the subway and say, 'Ooooh, you're funny!' And when she was done, I realized I was the only who got up and said, 'Thank you very much!'"

Funny story. I guess the story was meant to show that comedians are so needy of acknowledgment.

But then, isn't everyone?

Maybe the only reason the lady on the subway said all the other "Ooooh, you're funnys" was because – she just wanted more "Thank yous."

Thank yous are important.

(And just in case you don't have anyone to thank at any given moment, I'll tell you a quick story about the previously discussed Jimmy Durante. Every night, after each show, Jimmy would go to the nearest telephone, dial the letters G-O-D and say "Thank You.")

ROBIN WILLIAMS

On the Money

"When Mork & Mindy went off the air, I spent my time going door to door saying, 'Are there any job openings here that pay $40,000.00 a week?'"

– Robin Williams

Money is a strange thing. So many of us spend so much time thinking about it.

I remember all the great Borsht Belt comics doing lines about it:

Gene Baylos – *"I have enough money to last me the rest of my life – if I die Tuesday!"*
Joey Adams – *"I've saved my money for a rainy day – if it's more than a drizzle, I'm broke!"*
Billy Gray – *"They say 'Money Talks!'… to me it says, 'Good-bye!'"*
Jackie Clarke – *"Money isn't everything – credit is also important!"*

But every once in a while, a man you never met will come up to you and offer you $40,000.00 worth of goods or services – for free.

It was a Saturday night, and our little back-street comedy club was sold out. We were thrilled. This week, we would make money! What could be better than a sell out? We were about to see.

A car pulled up to the door and a man got out, inquiring about tickets. "We're sold out, sorry!" we said. He went back to the car, leaned into the passenger window with the news, and came back with an offer. "My friend says if you find us seats, he'll do a free show." We asked, "Who's your friend?" He said, "Robin Williams." We leaned into the passenger window. It was Robin Williams! We found seats. No charge.

Robin asked us to hide him away in a side room till he was on. He knew if the people recognized him the other comedians on the show wouldn't have a chance. There, in the private room, someone joked that we could never dream of being able to afford to have him perform at our little club. "My pleasure," he countered. "It's not about the money."

We were struggling comedians in a struggling comedy club. "Not about the money" wasn't a phrase we heard very often.

I flashed back to being 5 years old. A very old man named Mr. Micunis used to visit my grandfather every so often. I would hear the combination of Italian words and Yiddish words thrown into the otherwise English conversation. And when Mr. Micunis would come, he always gave me a shiny new quarter. I was always happy to see him. This day, he said, "Come here." He held out a shiny new quarter. "What do you see?" he asked. I said, "A quarter." "What else?" he asked. I said, "25 cents?" He said, "Do you see fingers? Do you see a hand? Do you see an arm? Do you see a person? Do you see this chair? The wall? The painting on the wall? The room? The world?" He smiled and pressed the quarter into my hand. "This is very important," he said. "Never just look at the money!"

My brain fast-forewarded a lot of years. Now I was a young comedian, in a broken-down car , with a duct-taped door, and no air-conditioning in 95 degree weather. I was going with a comedian friend, Robbie Roman, to a Jewish Senior Center somewhere in North Jersey. The agent had been very vague about the location till the contract was signed. The job wasn't for much money, and half-way there, I realized the gas and the tolls would eat up much of that.

When I got there, I got this "Who's he?" look from some of the seniors who had probably seen the greatest entertainers in the world in their day. So here I was, on a hot day, in front of a shirt-sleeved crowd, for very little money, wondering, "What am I doing with my life?" Soon I would know.

When I got on stage, the laughs came. And by the end of the show there was a standing ovation. My first. As I looked at the front row, there were three men in short sleeves standing and applauding. I saw, on their forearms, numbers tattooed. I knew what this meant. They were survivors of the death camps. All of a sudden, I couldn't hear the applause, I couldn't think of the money. I could only realize that if laughter could give these people, who had seen such horror, one hour of pleasure, I knew what I was doing with my life.

Back to Robin Williams. We told all the comics to cut their sets way short – Robin Williams was doing a 'guest set' for FREE! And when we introduced him, the audience response was – "Yeah, sure!" till they saw it was him! And then the place went nuts!

He bounded on stage with an energy that was contagious. And for the next 40 minutes, he did his thing.

There in the spotlight was an entertainer, doing it pretty much the way it's been done since the days of the court jester – the task was:

To give freely of your abilities.
To stand bravely, and be yourself.
To strive, working hard, till it came easily.
And always, to stop -- and enjoy.

Come to think of it, that's a fair representation of a happily lived life.

HENNY YOUNGMAN

Take My Advice, Please!

"My wife is on a new diet. Coconuts and bananas. Hasn't lost any weight, but boy can she climb trees!"

"I told my mother-in-law to make my home her home. She did – she sold it!"

"My furrier crossed a mink with a gorilla – beautiful coat, but the sleeves are too long!"

— Henny Youngman

Those may not be the hippest jokes ever written, but with Henny Youngman at the wheel, they always got a laugh. He delivered them like he believed in them. He delivered them like he enjoyed them. And it was because he really did! With a simple smile and a violin as a prop, Henny Youngman always looked like he was having fun up there. Sometimes he even laughed at his own jokes. It was the reason he was the "king" at what he did – one-liners.

When I was a kid, I would go anywhere to see a comedian. I sneaked into burlesque houses, sneaked into TV studios, sneaked into nightclubs – usually because I was under age. After the gatekeepers knew me, and that I was there to study, access was easier.

But the strangest place I've ever seen comedians perform was outside in the open air in front of the Art Museum in Philadelphia. The City Recreational Department had erected a flatbed truck stage on the Benjamin

Franklin Parkway, and the audience used the steps (the same ones Rocky ran up) as bleachers.

I saw several comedians bomb there!

And there's a real reason why most bombed. Comedy almost always requires intimacy. The closer you are to your audience, the more focused they can be. The closer they are to each other, the more contagious the laughter will be.

Can you imagine telling a joke to a friend across a football field? It's a little strained, a little forced. You can't see facial movements; you can't pick up subtleties! The wide-open spaces provide too many distractions.

The Art Museum steps provided soooo many distractions: trees, fountains, statues, wind, street noises, traffic, kids with balloons, guys selling pretzels.

Week after week I saw top comics bomb there. One, who is a household name, had a car backfire during his act. He said, "I know I'm not doing good, but don't shoot me!"
Then, on came Henny Youngman:

"I love this city! I solved the parking problem here. I bought a parked car!"

"I said to my friend, 'I don't understand gambling. One day I win – the next day I lose!' He said – 'Play every other day!'"

"You people are great – I want to take you home with me!"

There was a solid 40 minutes of non-stop laughter. What a job – the crowd loved him.

Why did Henny do so well with everything stacked against him? Well, there were a lot of reasons. Professionalism. Determination. Stamina. Material that only required a short attention span. But mostly it was what he told me after the show.

When this teenager waited around for him after the crowd cleared and cornered him outside his trailer and then asked him what I should do if I wanted to be a comedian, Henny said, "Don't let anybody or anything discourage you!"

And then he said, "Wanna see a picture of my Pride and Joy?"

He whipped out his wallet and showed me a photo – of a can of Pride furniture polish and a bottle of Joy dishwashing detergent!

He gave it to me. And it wasn't till years later I realized what the real message was. Against all odds, he had Pride in what he did, and he took Joy in doing it!

If you can put those two things into whatever you do – you've got any deterrent beat!

MOREY AMSTERDAM

The Joy in Your Job!

"So this guy works for the circus. His job is to take a shovel and broom, walk in the parade, and clean up behind the elephant! His friend says, 'That job is horrible. Why don't you quit?'

He says, 'What? And give up show business?'"

– Morey Amsterdam

Most of us spend about a third of our lives doing our jobs. It's important that our attitude reflect some joy found in those jobs. It's important that we get some joy from those jobs.

The last time I met Morey Amsterdam was at a rather strange job – at a strange time –two in the afternoon at a Boscov's department store in Plymouth Meeting, PA. The "job" was, as always, a show. And not so strange a place for Morey Amsterdam. He had "opened" every one of Boscov's department stores in America for the past twenty years as the "Ambassador of Laughter." The crowd always came to see him and his hilarious act – and today was no different. It was standing room only in the auditorium as Morey took the stage.

"Boscov's has been wonderful," he said. "They sent a police escort to get me! It was hard running between those motorcycles!"

Everywhere Morey went there was a show. So it had been for over 60 years, in two-a-day vaudeville, in nightclubs, hotels, radio, TV, movies, condominiums, cruise ships – anywhere there was a crowd. And anywhere

Morey Amsterdam went, there was a crowd. That's why Boscov's was thrilled to have him.

When we said hello, I reminded him of the first time we met. Almost twenty years before at The Downingtown Inn. He told me then, "I'm the luckiest guy around because I love what I do no matter where I do it. Because I hope my jokes make the world a happier place."

Not only was he a comedian, but he had long been a comedy writer. As a kid he had written for Will Rogers. How many people can say that?

Later, he'd write for Jack Benny, Robert Benchley, Bob Hope and hundreds more. He bragged, "Bob Hope knows me longer than he knows his wife!" Whenever a singer or a fellow comic needed a joke on a specific topic, a call went out to Morey Amsterdam. "Morey," they'd say, "do you have a joke about...?" He always did. He had a joke for everything.

He got a reputation as a "Human Joke Machine." In his own act, he often opened himself to the challenge of letting the audience suggest his topics. How appropriate that he'd gain probably his most lasting fame as fast-thinking joke writer Buddy Sorell on *The Dick Van Dyke Show*. "They were five of the happiest years of my life," he said. "At the time, most people had no idea how a writing staff came up with jokes, routines, sketches. It was the behind-the-scenes look that was fascinating."

During the meeting, I reminded him that twenty years before he had taught me a trick to "building" an act. A trick to "finding" the jokes. You break up a topic into its component parts. Let's say you want to do a routine about a guy getting married. Well, you've got marriage jokes. He's probably got to get a tuxedo, so you've got a men's clothing store joke. He's got to get a ring, so there's a jewelry store joke. There's a mother-in-law joke. There's a reception at a catering hall, so there's a food joke. There's dancing after, so there's a newest dance craze joke. Off to the honeymoon, there's an airplane joke, a lost luggage joke, a hotel joke, a bellboy joke. And once they get into the room ... well, if you can't think of some jokes for that, you shouldn't be a comedian!

What's that got to do with finding the "joy in your job?" Well, you find the "joy" the same way you find the "jokes."

As I watched Morey perform, I "broke down" the "job" of comedian into its "component parts." No matter where you do it, no matter what the venue, the basics are the same: You build an act, you get to meet people, you tell them jokes, you make the world a little nicer place. That's how Morey found the "joy" in his "job."

Anybody can do it with their job. There is joy in every job. (Unless what you do is hurtful or illegal.) Look for the joy in your job. Break it down into its component parts and ask – How does this make the world a little bit better place? How does it help society? How does it help even one person?

If you really break it down, there's definitely meaning, purpose and joy in every job.

A seventeen-year old taught me something once. (I say that because when you become an "adult," you never think a seventeen-year old can teach you anything. I learned better.)

I asked him if he had a job.

He said, "Yes, I work at McDonald's."

I said, "What do you make there?"

He said, "I make hamburgers."

I said, "No, I mean how much do they pay you?"

And he said, "I don't think about it that way. You see, I make hamburgers. And when I wrap them up and put them out, sometimes I look to see who gets them. Maybe it's a little kid. I follow him with my eyes. I wait to see him take the first bite. Sometimes they smile."

He said, "I make hamburgers, and I make kids smile. And for that, they pay me!"

Wow! That very mature seventeen-year old knew how to find the joy in his job.

Morey Amsterdam, in his 80's, loved doing those department store shows. What more could you ask for? It was all here – a great auditorium, great crowds, loud laughs, a stream of fans afterward asking for autographs. And two shows a day – like the old days in vaudeville. It was wonderful.

Morey Amsterdam passed away less than ten days after I last saw him. He was doing his job to the end. Down here, that is. I'm sure "up there" he's still doing it! Probably two-a-day!

> *"One day I met God ... He sneezed ... I didn't know what to say!"*

> – Morey Amsterdam

I told you he had a joke for everything!

DON RICKLES

Patience

"Being on this show is exciting. It's like sitting on a rowboat in the middle of a lake waiting for a carp to grab your worm!"

– Don Rickles

I never did understand fishing. Getting up so early, rowing out on a lake, baiting a hook, waiting for a bite, then rowing back, cleaning it, filleting it, breading it, and cooking it – just to eat it? Hey, I get impatient if there are more than three cars in the drive-thru line at McDonald's when I want a fish sandwich! I have a problem with patience. But Don Rickles taught me something about that.

It's hard to believe a time when there were no VCRs, no DVDs, but there was. People had to wait for their favorite show to be on, and be present when it aired. You couldn't just tape it and watch it when the mood struck you. If you missed it, you had to wait and hope for reruns. I don't know how we ever lived through that era. I hated it. We used to have to wait for a lot of things. We used to have to wait for food to cook in the oven, sometimes for hours. There were TV dinners, but even they took 20 minutes – because there were no microwaves. So we waited.

Our parents, now they really waited for things. They were children of the Depression. They waited in soup lines. They waited in ration lines. They waited for things to get better. And worked to make it happen. They had patience.

Their parents, wow, they waited to save enough money to come to this country. They waited for citizenship. They waited for jobs. They waited for social acceptance. Sometimes they waited to send for the rest of their family, so they could be together. They had patience!

In fact, if you go back far enough in part of my ethnic background, Moses waited 40 years to get through the desert. That's patience! (I couldn't even watch the movie *The Ten Commandments* without fast-forwarding through the commercials).

It's the era I grew up in, I guess. We have fast-food joints, fast cars, instant ice tea. If they don't deliver a pizza to your house in 30 minutes – it's free! There's even an 800 number to call if you need a mattress in an hour! Who needs a mattress in an hour? Do you all of a sudden realize – I'm gonna be tired in an hour – I need a mattress! The July issue of *Sports Illustrated* is out in June. They start decorating for Christmas in October. We don't mail if we can Fed Ex. And we don't Fed Ex if we can email. God forbid we should wait a whole day for anything.

While their culture taught our ancestors PATIENCE, our culture fosters our IMPATIENCE.

Anyway, what was I saying? Oh yes, I can't believe there was a time when there were no VCRs. It was the first time I ever appeared on TV. It was *The Maury Povich Show* (not the recent one, the one he had in the late '70s for Westinghouse). I was a young comic on with Don Rickles. I was thrilled. (Years before he had insulted me ringside at The Latin Casino. I was dating my wife. And if you've ever seen the size of my nose, you could imagine the type of insult. But to me a Don Rickles' personalized insult was like a medal of honor. I bragged about it forever.) Now I was going to be on TV with him, just for a minute or two – but on TV with Don Rickles – WOW!

When I started to talk to him, my mouth was going a mile a minute. And with a look on his face that I've only seen on severely constipated people, he said, "What is wrong with you? Slow down! What is it with these kids today? They're all in such a hurry!" It got a laugh, even from me. But he went on to talk about how in his day, in his career in fact, things took time to happen. And you waited for them. That was about all I could remember, because with the lights and the cameras and the excitement, it was all a blur. I couldn't wait to see it aired the next day on TV, to hear what he actually said.

And then on the way home I realized when it aired at 10 a.m., I wouldn't be anywhere near a TV! I had to be at a newspaper office to do an interview.

Well, I pushed the interview up to 9:00 and had a plan. As soon as the interview was over, I'd rush to the nearest TV four blocks away at the John Wanamaker's department store and catch the show. Well, forget the plans! The reporter showed up late, the interview ran late, and I ran to Wanamaker's. I ran into the store, ran up to a guard, and, out of breath, asked, "Where are the TV's?" They were downstairs, so I ran down the escalator (it wasn't going fast enough for me) and into the appliance department.

It was 10:10! I was worried I'd missed my segment. But by Divine Providence, I hit the wall of TVs, luckily all tuned to the right channel, just in time to see Maury Povich introduce me to Mr. Rickles. There it was on a hundred different TV screens, five rows high and twenty deep. Me and Don Rickles.

How ironic that Don Rickles (x 100) was repeating to a now-out-of-breath, rushed young man, "What is wrong with you? Slow down! What is it with these kids today? They're all in such a hurry."

He spoke in detail about seeing young comics at the Improvs and The Comedy Stores in such a hurry to become stars, but not taking the time to hone their skills. Some things just take time. Art is one. Ask Michelangelo. Seven years to do a ceiling? And he wasn't even union.

It took Rickles years. After the War, he went to the American Academy of Dramatic Arts, had as classmates Charles Bronson and Jack Klugman. But acting didn't work out, so he became a comic. A dozen years in small clubs and strip joints as comic-emcee prepared him for better rooms. More years coast to coast before Sinatra discovered him at The Slate Brothers Club, where he said his dressing room was in an alley. Another 10 years toiling in the lounges in Las Vegas before anyone would "take a chance on him" for TV. That someone was Johnny Carson. And so, with *The Tonight Show,* Don Rickles became an "overnight sensation" – after 20 years of work and patience! (Later, the acting would come around too, with great parts from *The Rat Race* to *Casino.*)

Yet, he said that the success was so much sweeter for having endured the wait. And so much more appreciated than if it had come quickly.

I'd come to see it later, again and again, especially in the comedy clubs that I was affiliated with for so long. Young, talented comics who gave up after a year or two or three, because they couldn't wait. But other comics, who weren't as good, but who got good by hanging in, and working, and waiting – made it!

Don Rickles was right, with patience, everything is sweeter when it comes around.

The food tastes better when you smell it cooking for hours. The iced tea is more quenching when you have to wait for it to steep. The bed feels better when you've waited all day to climb into it. The magazine is more exciting to read when you've waited for it all month. And Christmas, well, it just can't come before December 25th.

Some things are worth the wait.

Some things are worth more because of the wait.

Ask any fisherman.

Or better yet – go fishing!

SHECKY GREENE

Living in the Present

"Trying to make people laugh in a casino is very different.
Some guy just lost thirty thousand dollars at craps, and a pit
boss says, 'Hey, you wanna see a funny kid?'
The guy says, 'Oh yeah, my bus don't leave for another hour!'
The pit boss says, 'You're taking a bus home, sir?'
The guy says, 'No, I was gonna lie under it!'"

– Shecky Greene

Shecky Greene was a legend in Las Vegas. It was the only place you could see him live. So on his first East Coast tour, you bet I was the first one to buy the first tickets for the first night of his week at the Valley Forge Music Fair. I would have bought tickets for the whole week, but I was a college student and tickets were expensive.

As it turned out, I didn't have to buy tickets for the entire week. After opening night, I wrote a letter and sent it backstage. Shecky was kind enough not only to invite me to his dressing room, but also to tell the house manager, "See this kid, let him in free every night – and backstage after!" Nice man. He knew I was a comedian in the making and eager to learn.

The first thing I learned was that every night was a little different. The audience was the variable. Some crowds laughed longer and louder than others at the same routines. Some nights it was easy; some nights he had to work a little harder. But always he had to stay "in the present." And that was part of the enjoyment!

He told me his Las Vegas lounge years prepared him for that. Two, sometimes three shows a night. And the gambling audiences ran the gamut from happy winners to lonesome losers. And every show was a crapshoot. You played to what was out there. You played the hand you were dealt. And you stayed in the present. It kept you on your toes.

He told me you go out there realizing that every show is its own entity, and every crowd its own entity. This crowd doesn't know that the last show might not have been great, and they don't care that the next show might be colossal. *All that matters to them is this show.* The comedian has to be the same way.

You can't wallow in the sorrow of a past show or worry about the quality of a future show – you can only do your best with this show. And an hour later – you've got to do it all over again.

Somewhere I heard that neither sorrow nor worry can exist because of the present.

Think of it. Everything we're sorry for - is what happened in the past. And everything we're worried about – is what will happen in the future. While it's good to learn from past failures and be concerned with future plans, we can eliminate 99% of our useless sorrow and worry simply by focusing on the present. Not the present as it relates to the past, or the present as it hinges on the future – but just the present!

If you eliminate all the effort of that sorrow and worry, you'll have a lot more energy.

And for those of us who spend a lot of hours wallowing – we'll have a lot more time, too. Time and energy to enjoy this moment – and be happy!

So Shecky Greene taught me how to live in the moment. Interesting that one of the most "in the moment" things I ever did was because of him.

Here I was at my little after college part-time job, a year or so after meeting Shecky. I had seen him on TV, the night before, promoting an appearance at The Westbury Music Fair in Connecticut. On a whim, I picked up the phone, called Connecticut, got the box office, had a ticket held in my name, told my boss I'd be back tomorrow, got on a train and rode three hours to Westbury. Once there, I took a cab to the box office, asked what hotel Shecky was at, called and told him what I'd done, and he directed me to his dressing room/trailer, where he'd be in a half hour or so. He welcomed me and was wonderful.

That night, following country singer Diana Trask, Shecky held court on stage "in the round." Two thousand people were roaring laughing as he pulled out all the stops. Here was Shecky, joking, singing, dancing, doing impressions, props, dialects, and the audience was convulsing with laughter. But ringside, he caught sight of one guy, and said, "Sir I notice you're not laughing. I've been doing this act for 20 years, and I just realized, you're right, this stuff's not funny!' And the audience roared again, as Shecky stayed in the moment.

ROSIE O'DONNELL
No Offense Taken!

"When you get famous, people say strange things to you. Once a lady said – 'I hope you're not insulted – but do you know you look like Rosie O'Donnell?' Insulted? Well, I wasn't – but I am now!"

– Rosie O'Donnell

The lesson, and it took me a long time to learn it, was – Be Slow To Take Offense! (Because there's so much to be offended by, it'll all make you crazy!)

I know it's easier said than done. People are sensitive, egos are fragile, tempers flare, hostilities build, but if you can count to 10 you can lower your blood pressure considerably. (Early in my career, in an angry phone call to an agent about something, I was told I should have counted to 10 before I called. I said, "I counted to 100 – you should have heard me at 10!") I've learned since.

It was a hundred years ago. (Well, at least 75 years, before Rosie joined the ranks of hit talk show hosts). Rosie O'Donnell and I were performing at a restaurant called Lulu Wellington's in Warminster, PA. Nice place. Rosie had driven in from New York with a friend, Margaret Smith (who would later star in *That '80s Show*), who filled out the bill. I won't say what the three of us were making, but if we pooled our money – maybe we could have afforded a meal there! (But we weren't complaining, this was a cash job! Real money. And like most newcomers, we were grateful just for the stage time.) So, we weren't complaining.

Well, actually, we were complaining, in a fun way. Before the show, we started to trade stories of insults, indignities and various affronts we'd suffered for our "art." We all had them. As young comics, lucky to be working anywhere, we weren't always treated even as well as second-class citizens. But we'd learned to laugh it off. And it made us stronger.

I love *Ziggy*. I saw a great *Ziggy* cartoon once that said, *"I've learned the secret of Happiness – I've learned how to enjoy Misery!"*

So we all had our stories. And as humbling as they were, they were funny. I won't tell you their stories; that would be ungentlemanly. But I'll tell you mine. It was the story of a "food gig." For those not accustomed to the parlance of comedians, a "gig" is a job or a show. A "food gig" is a job that doesn't always pay cash, but the establishment does give you a meal.

Well, a week before working with Rosie and Margaret, I had taken this "food gig" with three other comics, at a place in Philadelphia better left unnamed. When I sat down with the other comics to order, I decided to have the chopped steak. Not a high-priced item, somewhat medium-priced, but it's what I was in the mood for. The waitress took my order, but before she took the other three, she went back to the kitchen. I had explained to her that we were the comedians, and in lieu of pay, our meals were complimentary. (I felt like I was carrying a sign that said – *"Will Work for Food!"*)

In a minute or so, I saw her talking to the owner. She looked embarrassed. She came back to the table and said, "I'm sorry, the owner said – comedians can't have meat!"

Comedians Can't Have Meat!

How nice!

When I told Rosie the story, I said that would be my epitaph, "Comedians Can't Have Meat!" She said, "Oh, no – it's mine now – I'm taking it!" We laughed in a way that only two "survivors" can. We had that someday-we'll-be-able-to-eat-in-the-best-of-places attitude. And we laughed.

We had learned to laugh in the face of adversity. We learned to be slow to take offense. It would be a well-serving coat of armor. It would make us downright invulnerable. And like *Ziggy,* it would preserve our happiness.

A sign at a comedy club entrance once said –
"Check Your Sensitivity At The Door!"

Not a bad idea. There are a million things to be sensitive about, a million things to be hurt by. And if you're too sensitive, you're going to be hurt by all of them. And often needlessly.

You see, I really believe that most people are decent. Now, they might be rude for a second, or discourteous for a moment, or cranky for an hour, or selfish for a decade. But for the most part, they're not malicious, not trying to deliberately offend you. Often they don't even know they have. If you call it to their attention, they'll apologize.

Also, you have to consider the source. Maybe the guy just had a bad experience, and you're the next person he meets, so he's taking it out on you.

A personal example:

Once I was booked to do a show at a hotel. I was given a hotel room that was way below shabby. It had no phone, no TV, and no carpeting. My gut reaction was to say – "That's it, I'm leaving!" But instead, I politely asked, "Why such a shabby room?" The owner said, "The last comic trashed his room!" I told the owner if he'd give me a regular room, he could have his staff inspect it before I checked out, and if there were any irregularities, he could put the charge on my credit card. Not only did he give me a nice room, but every time I played a return engagement there, I always got one of the best accommodations in the house.

I've found that most people are nice and can be reasoned with. A few, though, are jerks. And there's not much you can do about them. They've probably been jerks for a long time. The most you can do is point it out to them, if reasoning doesn't work. I have a friend who carries these little cards that he bought in a novelty store. He hands them out on rare occasions when it's appropriate. They say:

> *"You have just offended me.*
> *This card is chemically treated.*
> *In fifteen minutes your (blank) will fall off!"*

(I won't tell you which body part is named in the blank; suffice it to say he carries different cards for men and women.)

But better not to get all bent out of shape for those few. And when you encounter the "few," go over, under, around, or through them. Or avoid them altogether. Be slow to take offense, because honestly there are people who don't have a clue what they're saying or doing.

Case in point: One night after a great show at Caesars Cove Haven Resort in the Poconos, a little white-haired lady, who appeared to be about 70 years old, came up to me and said, "Young man, I want you to know something. You are the best comedian I've ever seen. I watch all these comedians on cable TV, and they sing and dance, and do impressions, and play instruments... and they don't make me laugh. But tonight you made me laugh with no talent whatsoever!"

I swear she meant it as a compliment!

RED BUTTONS

Laugh It Off!

"When I was in Hollywood, accepting an Academy Award for my role in Sayonara, who knew that some day...some day...I would be performing here, here, in Flushing, Queens! ...But wherever there's a show, I'll be there...Always there... In Beverly Hills, at The Annual Guess Who Your Father Is Meeting, I was there...In Osaka , at a Reunion of Japanese Kamikaze Pilots, I was there...In the garment center of New York, at The Convention of Business Partners Who Trust Each Other – I was alone, but I was there!

–Red Buttons

There's a big difference between not taking offense at a situation, and laughing it off. Laughing it off is definitely a higher state of happiness.

The first time I met Red Buttons, I was six years old, and my father took a picture of us together at a new car dealership picnic, where Mr. Buttons was booked to "appear." Not do his act, just appear, take pictures, sign autographs. Not exactly a normal gig, but for a ton of money, because he was a major TV star. His TV show was a hit, his song *Strange Things Are Happening: The Ho-Ho Song* was a hit. He was as hot as could be.

We met again 20 years later, after he sent me a very kind thank you letter for reviewing his show at the Valley Forge Music Fair. The show was *Burlesque-U.S.A.*, a review paying homage to The Golden Days of Burly-Q. Fitting that Red Buttons would be the star, since he got his start in the art as a teenager among old time baggy pants comics, billed as "the only comedian in burlesque with teeth". (And Burlesque in the 1920s, '30s and '40s wasn't the pole-dancing, raunchy remnant that exists today. It was, in fact, just a risqué variety show: 60% comedy sketches, 5% variety acts, 15% chorus girls, and 20% teasing strip teasers who wound up wearing more clothes than you'd see at the beach today on the 4th of July. As for the naughty comedy sketches, they'd be PG in comparison to the R, X, and XXX comedy you can see on TV now). And what's ironic is, when New York's Mayor LaGuardia closed down Minsky's Burlesque for the good of public morality, Red Buttons was on stage at the time. "Sometimes", he said, "you just have to laugh!"

Red reminisced about all the great comics that came from burlesque. He spring boarded his career from the boards of Minsky's to his own TV show, headlining in nightclubs, starring in movies, and doing innumerable guest appearances on every show from *Ed Sullivan* to *The Tonight Show*, *The Dean Martin Show* to *Roseanne*. There were so many burlesque alumni who became stars of movies, TV, and theater. There was Bert Lahr, Will Rodgers, Fanny Brice, Abbott & Costello, Bobby Clark, Danny Thomas, Phil Silvers, Jackie Gleason, Pinky Lee, Pigmeat Markham ("Here Come the Judge"), Jack Albertson (of *Chico and The Man*), Joe DeRita (Curly Joe of *The 3 Stooges*), Joey Faye, Herbie Faye, Vinnie Faye, and Mickey Deems (perennial character actors), Rags Ragland, Billy Gilbert, Ben Turpin, and Leon Errol (Hollywood favorites), Joe E. Ross (of *Car 54, Where Are You?*), B.S. Pulley (from Broadway's *Guys & Dolls*), Irv Benson (aka Sidney Spritzer from *The Milton Berle Show*), as well as a ton of dyed-in-the-wool burlesquers like "Slapsie Maxie" Furman, Billy "Zoot" Reed, Billy "Cheese & Crackers" Hagan, Lou Ascol, Bert Gehan, Jo-Jo Jordan, Tommy "Moe" Raft, Benny "Wop" Moore, Steve Mills, Mac Dennison, Harry Connelly, Hermie Rose, Billy Foster, Bert Carr, and so many more who spent their lives in bubble noses and baggy pants. I saw them all in their later years, still sharp as tacks & polished as diamonds on stage. Great comedians all!

So then I showed Mr. Buttons the picture of us from two decades before. He told me, as a kid in the business, agents booked him anywhere they could: supermarket openings, block parties, fire houses, picnics, anywhere, and not for the kind of big bucks he was getting when we took that picture. The joke used to be, "Send 5 pounds of potato salad and Red

Buttons." Now, as an Academy Award winner, he could really laugh off those early, crazy jobs.

In my starting out days, I told him I also had a number of jobs I could only "laugh off." There was the "pool party" where my "stage" was a plank stretched across the swimming pool . There was the bikers' picnic where the stage was directly in front of a row of Port-A-Pottys. We all have those stories, harrowing at the time, but laughable later. As I traded stories with Mr. Buttons, I had to tell him my two favorites:

It was my first "good money" job. I was 21. Three nights: Thursday, Friday, Saturday. It was billed as a Las Vegas Show (even though it was in South Philadelphia). It was a band, a singer, and me. We weren't given a show time, so we got there early. When the promoter opened up the doors to the show room, it was quite a revelation. We were looking at a totally functional, totally illegal casino. Crap tables, roulette wheels, poker tables, and ladders where "pit bosses" sat to survey and supervise. Hefty stakes, $100 limits.

"What time would you like us to start?" we asked. "Don't worry about it," was the answer. "Here's the deal. We put up posters in the neighborhood that say *Las Vegas Show*. That tells everybody that it's really a casino night. Nobody comes for a show. But if we get word that we're going to get raided, we cover up the tables, send everybody down front, and while the cops are here, you do your show, until they leave. So if there's no raid, we don't need a show – but don't worry, you still get paid."

Well, Thursday, no raid, no show. Friday, no raid, no show. Saturday, the boss has an attitude. He says, "You guys have been freeloading long enough. Tonight you do two shows, 10 and 12." Fair enough. The 10pm show, the band plays, nobody dances, people are playing poker, shooting craps, watching the roulette wheel. The singer sings, nobody listens, they're playing poker, shooting craps, watching the roulette wheel. But, undaunted, this 21-year-old comic is determined to get them. I start pounding out jokes, and they start watching, and laughing, and applauding. I'm a hit! I do my 15 minutes, and as I walk off stage, a guy with no neck points a finger in my face that looks like a cannon. With a voice that sounds like he's been gargling with gravel he says, "HEY FUNNYBOY!" I said "Yes". He says, "You made them laugh, didn't you?" I said, "Yes". He said, "You know what they weren't doing while they were laughing?" I said, "No". He said, "They weren't loosing money! ... Next show, you don't be so funny, OK. 'Cause if you are, I'm gonna rip the microphone outta the wall!"

Later, I'd think, "Welcome to Show business" and I'd laugh it off.

Story number two: Ten years later in my career. I'm a "seasoned performer." Ha! Thought I'd seen everything. I was a little famous in Philly. Picture in the paper every week, name in the columns. An agent calls, says that a client has seen my act and wants to book me for a banquet. Big money. I show up for the job at a downtown restaurant and am directed to the upstairs banquet room. They open the doors, and I see that the room is as wrong for a show as a room can be. It is the configuration of one lane in a bowling alley. The room is 6 feet wide and 150 feet long. There are 38 round tables in a single file line. The first table is twenty feet from the stage (there's a dance floor, of course) and table 38 is in another time zone. There are no stage lights, no sound system. I'm thinking, they can't see me, they can't hear me - it couldn't be any worse! Wanna bet?

The client comes in and greets me happily, he says, "We've seen your act and we think you're going to be great. One thing, though, if you pick volunteers from the audience, we want you to only pick people at table 38". I say, "Well, that's very far away. Why only from table 38?" He says, "Because they're the only ones who speak English."

We laughed.

And then Red Buttons trumped me with a story of his own. He was a new comer in the business. He only did a 10-minute act in those days. Three Jewish jokes and a song parody about a Jewish tailor - *Sam, You Made the Pants Too Long*, in a thick Yiddish dialect.

Well, he shows up for this job, it's a men's group. He tells his first Jewish joke – Nothing! ...Tells the second Jewish joke – again, NOTHING! ... Now he tells the third one and there's murmuring in the crowd. He starts singing with a Yiddish accent, "Pants are dragging, slowly dragging," and a beer bottle flies in front of his face and hits the wall. They're throwing things at him. He ducks under the piano and crawls off stage.

Later the agent called and apologized. He had booked him at an inappropriate function. It was a Nazi Bund Meeting.

Sometimes you just have to "laugh it off."

MAXIE, PINKY, AND SEÑOR WENCES
WISHES & DREAMS

An Old Burlesque Bit:
1ˢᵗ Comic: "I love baseball. I eat, sleep, and dream baseball.
Last night I dreamt I was at a ballgame!"
2ⁿᵈ Comic: "Last night I dreamt I was out with two beautiful
blondes!"
1st Comic: "You dreamt you were out with TWO beautiful
blondes? Why didn't you call me?"
2ⁿᵈ Comic: "I did. They said you were at the ballgame!"

When I was a kid, I would stand in front of the TROC Burlesque Theater in Philadelphia and wait for comedian Max Furman. We'd walk to Gansky's Deli and he'd tell me of the glory days of Burlesque. The days when it had class and elegance. Years later I would do the Joel Spivak TV Show with him. I literally saw him cry at what burlesque had become. He dreamed of the old days and wished it could be that way again. He got his wish. He lived his dream. He was later cast in a co-starring role in the Broadway show *Sugar Babies* with Mickey Rooney and Ann Miller, which relived those former days in all their glory. I was so glad he got his dream.

I remember, as a kid, staring at the ten-foot-high pictures of comedians and showgirls outside the TROC, dreaming what it must have been like inside. I couldn't get in at age ten, but I so wished I could be on that stage. I remember thinking, Abbott & Costello appeared on that stage! I would get my wish, too. Years later, the TROC would be a Chinese movie theater. But for one night only, it was donated to The Variety Club to do a fundraiser to send needy kids to camp. I found myself lucky enough (thanks to friend and *Philadelphia Daily News* columnist Stu Bykofsky) to be on stage with fellow comic Maria Merlino, trading jokes almost as corny as the one above. Dreams and wishes are important. They can come true.

As a kid, I watched *The Pinky Lee Show* on TV. Pinky had the reputation of being "the cleanest comic in burlesque," so giving him a TV show was no problem for the networks. As a kid, in the '50s, I wished I could have met him. As a teen I remember wishing I could go to The Broadway Theater in Pitman, N.J., where Pinky was appearing in Ann Corio's *Here It Is, Burlesque*. Not to be – again, too young. But in the '80s, I got to meet Pinky at Lilly Langtry's in Valley Forge, PA. He had just finished tap dancing on stage, while joking and playing the xylophone. As he walked toward me, he was limping. I said, "Pinky, what's wrong?" He said, "I hurt my leg last week." I said, "But you were just tap dancing up there". He said, "Well, I'm not going to let *them* know!"

That's called being a pro.

I told him how I'd wished I could have gone to Pitman twenty years before. He said, "I think it's still there." I'd get my wish. Five years later I'd be headlining (thanks to friend and producer Jonathan) in *Good Ole Vaudeville* – at The Broadway Theater, Pitman, N.J. Hang on to your wishes. Sometimes it takes years.

The Ed Sullivan Show was probably where everyone first saw five minutes of Señor Wences, the ventriloquist who made a puppet of his fist, "For you easy - for me Difficult," and talked to a dignified head in a box, "S'all Right – S'all Right." I would have gone to the ends of the earth to see his whole act. And I almost did.

When my wife Suzanne wanted to go to Europe, I made her a deal. I'd heard that the only place you could see Señor Wences was at The Crazy Horse Saloon in Paris. He'd been booked there for maybe a dozen years, and now, in his late eighties, he was still in this Parisian revue nightly. So the deal was, when we get to Paris, we have to go see Señor Wences.

When we got to The Hotel Arcade, before we even got to our room, I was with the concierge checking on The Crazy Horse Show. Big disappointment. He was no longer in it. Retired? Or worse, passed away? No one knew. "Oh well," I thought, "I came all this way."

When we got home two weeks later, we realized we'd forgotten to stop newspaper delivery. There were fourteen papers piled at the door. As I looked in the entertainment section, I saw an ad, appearing at Lilly Langtry's - five minutes from where we lived - was Señor Wences. You *know* where I was the next night!

Lilly's was an ultra elegant Victorian restaurant/theater, opulent in every way. It was the kind of place a comedy club comic like me couldn't get booked into, but as a customer I reveled in the fact that I finally got to see the entire Señor Wences act, truly a skilled work of art. A few years later (thanks to friend and comic-magician Jim Daly), I was invited to Señor Wences 93rd birthday party. (Señor Wences lived to be 103, and his classic act is carried on today by ventriloquist Michelle LaFong.) When I told him the story of my trip from halfway around the world to literally up the street to see him, he couldn't help but laugh. I told him how impressed I was with seeing him at the ornate Lilly Langtry's Theater. He said, "You may be there one day." I smiled and said "Thank You." And he signed my invitation "Remember your friend, Señor Wences." A few years later, (thanks to friend and comedian Big Daddy Graham) I would appear in Greg Thompson's *Celebrations on Ice* - at Lilly Langtry's.

Hang on to those wishes and dreams. They are important parts of your life. They can be fulfilled. Sometimes you pray your way into them. Sometimes you work your way into them. Sometimes you back your way into them. Sometimes they come as a gift from a friend. Sometimes they fall in your lap. But don't ever forget them. Go out and get them.

THE MYSTERY COMEDIAN

?

This was the hardest chapter to include, for two reasons:

First, it took me years to realize and accept that the advice within was legitimate. But when I finally did, I knew I couldn't justify leaving this chapter out.

Second, because the comedian who gave me this great piece of advice is the only one in the book I won't identify. I won't, because along with the advice, this "mystery comedian" told me a very personal, very confidential story that I don't feel comfortable retelling. Just know that it was about a very hurtful experience – and he only told it to me to drive home his two-word piece of advice.

So there will be no story, no comedian and no joke leading into this chapter, just his advice: "Forgive Everything."

Now, I know what you're thinking. The same thing I thought --
"But what if…"
FORGIVE EVERYTHING
"How about…"
FORGIVE EVERYTHING
"But you don't…"
FORGIVE EVERYTHING

Easier said than done. Much easier.

You may not be ready to forgive everything… you may not be willing to forgive everything… you may not be able to forgive everything… now… but maybe someday!

Here's what you do. Write those two words – FORGIVE EVERYTHIG – on a 3x5 card and put it in a place where you have to see it every day. Put it on your dressing mirror, in your bathroom, wherever. At first it will be upsetting. Then it will be annoying. Then it will be ridiculous. Then you'll see it and say, "Impossible." Then you'll see it and say, "It might help." And one day you'll see it and say "I understand." And one day you'll say "I must." And then one day you'll say "I CAN." On that day, a thousand-pound weight will be lifted from your body.

Now, "Forgiving" doesn't mean that if a man blows up your house, you go to him with a stick of dynamite, a match and your new address just to prove you trust him. He may not deserve your trust; he may not even want it. We're not talking about "him" here. He has his own issues. We're talking about YOU.

YOU eventually have to dump all the anger, resentment, fear, guilt and frustration caused by the event – and the only way to do that is to FULLY "FORGIVE EVERYTHING."

It took me 18 years to realize that, and I wish I could have shortened that period, because every day would have meant a day, a week, a month, a year sooner that I would have been free. I can't shorten it for you. When it comes, it comes. But keep those two words "FORGIVE EVERYTHING" written down, so that when the time comes, you'll be ready.

You'll be ready to let go of the rancor that has enveloped your life. You'll be ready to let go of the hate. And another really amazing thing will happen. You know how we all have that one thing (or more) that we regret having done, and you wish people would forgive you, but you don't know if they can, because after all, there's something that even you can't forgive? (Was that a run on sentence?) Well, the day that you can "FORGIVE EVERYTHING" is the day you'll feel like everyone can FORGIVE YOU, TOO! Another thousand-pound rock lifted.

Look for any reason in the world to forgive them. Forgive them because they're idiots. Forgive them because they're misguided. Forgive them because they don't know any better. But DO IT FOR YOUR SAKE! And do it in your own way, and in your own time.

How will you know it's time? OK, I will give you a joke… and I can do it because I'm part Italian:

> *"What's Italian Alzheimer's?*
> *That's when you forget everything – but a grudge!"*

When you can read that joke and laugh, you may be ready! You'll realize how hurtful to YOU a grudge is.

"FORGIVE EVERYTHING"

And then, as my friend, comedian Dom Irrera says, "FOGGETABOUDIT!"

FREDDIE ROMAN

Tradition

Two men meet on the street.
One says, "Rappaport, you've changed so much. Look at you. You lost weight.
You got a face lift. You got a hair transplant. I wouldn't know it was you!"
The other fella says, "I'm not Rappaport"
First fella says, "Oy, even your name you changed!"

…That's an old joke. I love the old jokes. And I tell them in the
tradition of the great storytellers: Myron Cohen, Jackie Miles, Menasha
Skulnik, so many more, because I refuse to let these stories die!"

— Freddie Roman

The story above is such a traditional Jewish joke, there's even a Broadway play with the set up as the title – *I'm Not Rappaport* (Writer's note: for Gentiles, the punch line should read, "Wow, you even changed your name!")

The first time I saw Freddie Roman was, I believe, his TV debut. Mike Douglas introduced him and said, "I saw this young man at a *TV Guide* dinner, and he had such bright, clever, new material, I had to have him on my show." And it proved true. Freddie had some of the freshest, most original material ever. Years later, actress Jaclyn Smith would introduce him to then President Reagan and the audience at Ford's Theater as, "The noblest Roman of them all". And again, he'd regale this prestigious crowd with sharp, original material.

So why, in his act, would he take time to include a half-dozen classic stories? The answer: Tradition! As he said, "I refuse to let these stories die!"

I knew I liked Freddie Roman. I too loved re-telling the classic jokes. It was easy for me to do in the "traditional" places like Palumbo's, Torano's, The Downingtown Inn, and The Pines Hotel in The Catskills. But I would even sneak in a few at comedy clubs. And they always worked.

(Oooh, a side story: I was booked by Vin D'Amato, a great friend and agent, into The Pines Hotel in The Catskills. My first of many times there. I show up at three in the afternoon, and the crowd is having a party in the lobby. The social director announces, "Tonight is Big Band Night, with a 22-piece big band" The crowd applauds. "And," he says, "a Comedian." The crowd starts booing! BOOING! Why are they booing? Do they hate comedians? What's going on here?

I go over to the social director. I tell him, "I'm the comedian – why are they booing?" He says, "Maybe you should just go home. Don't worry, we'll pay you." I said, "What happened?" He says, "We had a comedian Monday night so dirty, the whole audience walked out. Tuesday, I told the comedian to be clean, he was, but he wasn't funny! Half the audience walked out! They really don't want a comedian tonight."

I said, "Don't worry, we'll have fun." In the five hours that transpired between then and show time, every time the social director & I crossed paths, he said, with a worried look, "Are you sure?"

That night, I peppered my regular act extra heavy with the "traditional" jokes. Great jokes. Old jokes. Jokes that were written before I was born. And I got a standing ovation. One patron said, "You saved our vacation. We were ready to sue this place for our money back! You saved them from a lawsuit." And I had a ball, because there's something wonderful about going back to tradition.)

Traditions are warm and wonderful and comfortable. They're a port in the storm of the sometimes rocky sea of change. They're a life line to the past. Something tried and true. They're a friendly face that you instantly recognize. A memory you'd almost forgotten.

After all, what would the year be like if you didn't have fireworks on the 4TH of July, or a tree at Christmas, a menorah at Hanukkah, a Mother's Day in May, a Father's Day in June, Halloween in October, or a turkey on Thanksgiving? Traditions all. And ones that make you feel stable and secure.

To quote another Broadway play, "Without tradition, our lives would be as shaky as…as… a Fiddler on the Roof."

For a while, before I was The Professor of Fun™, I was billed as "The Last Catskill Comic in America," and doing an act filled with classic jokes and stories. So you know that when Freddie Roman (by now Dean of The Friars) created, hosted, and starred in *The Catskills on Broadway*, I was there to review it for my newspaper column. It was a wonderful show, steeped in the traditions of the mountain resort area in upstate New York, where vacationers went for the summer to play tennis, golf, swim, boat, eat sumptuous meals by day, and enjoy a new stage show every night, always with a comedian. (Comedians like Jerry Lewis, Jack Carter, Jan Murray, Buddy Hackett, Sid Caesar, and Danny Kaye all got their start there.) In *The Catskills on Broadway*, Freddie Roman, along with Marilyn Michaels, Dick Capri, and Mal Z. Lawrence, relived the traditions of "The Mountains." The show ran for years, touring with Freddie as host and sometimes guests, Louise DuArt, Stewie Stone, Corbett Monica, Frankie Pace, Sammy Shore and more. Keeping "the tradition" alive.

At every show, whether in Vegas, Atlantic City, Miami, or elsewhere, Freddie Roman would be on stage mixing great current events material about family, and kids, condominiums, commercials, and dieting, with classic jokes in an orator's style:

A 95-year-old man marries a 91-year-old woman. On their honeymoon night she says, "Sam, would you like to come up stairs and make love?" He says, "Sylvia, make up your mind – I can't do both!"

A little boy says to his grandmother, "Grandma, I have to pee." She says, "Honey, don't say that in public, it's very embarrassing. We'll make up a code word. If you have to do that say – Grandma, I have to whisper!…I'll know what you mean." No one tells Grandpa. A week later Grandpa is lying on the couch. *The little boy says, "Grandpa I have to whisper." Grandpa says, "Fine, whisper in Grandpa's ear!"*

A couple is married for 50 years. The wife passes away. They're at the funeral. The pallbearers pick up the casket, head toward the door. The casket bumps against the wall. From inside there comes a moan. They open it up, she's alive. The husband says, "It's a miracle." They go home. They're married 10 more years. Again the wife passes away. Again a funeral. Again they pick up the casket. And as the pallbearers head toward the door, the husband yells, "Watch out for the wall!"

Freddie would continue the tradition of telling those great stories in movies like *Sweet Lorraine* and the PBS special, *Now That's Funny!* with Jack Carter, Professor Irwin Corey, John Byner, Bill Dana, Charlie Callas, Dick Capri, Mal Z., and Paul Reiser. Great old stories. And every time I think of them, the old "traditions" make me feel complete. Old traditions – they're wonderful.

Now, that's not to say you shouldn't start "new traditions," as well. New traditions can be just as wonderful. But, most importantly, keep traditions, old and new. They make you feel warm inside.

SAMMY DAVIS JR.

Sanctuary

*"When I go on the road, I don't pack luggage,
I just put a handle on my house!"*

– Sammy Davis Jr.

OK, you're saying Sammy Davis Jr. wasn't a comedian. Well, as maybe the greatest entertainer of my generation, he was a singer/dancer/musician/actor/impressionist and he knew his way around a joke well enough to be a comedian. He could hold his own adlibbing with the best. And if you want to see his comedy skills, watch old episodes of *Laugh-In*. So, as a comedian, I say he qualifies. And he once gave a great piece of advice, "Surround yourself with the things that make you happy, the things that bring you peace, the things you love."

Sammy, even on the road, carried a collection of photos of family and friends that he'd set up in any hotel room, to make it feel like home. And with it a collection of "travel with" books, records, and tapes, that could transform the barest room into a sanctuary. A comfortable place.

Books, records, and tapes. I know about that. Newspaper stories have called my "office" a mini comedy museum. Framed pictures of comedians, memorabilia, over 800 joke books, 1,500 plus comedy records and tapes, and over 3,600 hours of stand-up videos are neatly arranged in 500 square feet. It's my sanctuary of sorts.

How'd I start collecting? Well, aside from the comedy albums I'd purchased as a teenager, it all started one night at The Golden Lion Pub in

New York. It was a weekly comedy class where Irving Dalvin got newbies like myself, George Wallace (yes, the now King of Las Vegas George Wallace), Rick Overton (then of Overton & Sullivan), Merle Exit, Artie Capp, Chuck Rizzo, Andy Lamberti and more to flex our muscles and spread our wings.

We'd pretty much just perform for each other, critiquing ourselves along the way. Some nights we'd have guests like Rick Newman of Catch A Rising Star. This was one of those nights. The guest was Leopold Fectner. I'd read about him in *TV Guide*. They called him "The Man Who Never Laughed." He had been a lifelong collector of humor. He had a library of joke books, cartoons, humor magazines. There wasn't a joke he hadn't heard at least five variations of. Hardy ever laughed anymore. I was determined to make him laugh, and I did. After, we spoke.

He told me how important he believed humor was. He told me how much good it could do. And he told me he had been a collector of joke books as a youth in pre-Nazi Germany. When the Nazis began burning books, he knew it was time to pack up and smuggle his books out of Europe and into America.

I couldn't get that scenario out of my mind.

Coming home that night, in Penn Station, I bought my first joke book.

I now have over 800 joke books, neatly arranged amid photos and comedy memorabilia. There's Jimmy Durante's hat, Soupy Sales' tie, a Leroy Neiman painting of Henny Youngman, a program from Señor Wences' 93rd birthday luncheon, a collection of Tommy Cooper props, press clippings, posters, hundreds of photos. I look around and feel comfortable there.

And in a special place, a framed coin that says, "Peace & Love – Sammy Davis Jr."

GEORGE CARLIN
Other Stuff

"Your house is nothing more than a place to keep your stuff – while you go out and get more stuff! And sometimes you've gotta move. Got to get a bigger house. Why? Too much stuff!"

– George Carlin

Anyone will tell you that one of the keys to happiness is to simplify. Watch the TV shows about hoarders, and you'll learn to keep the good "stuff," but get rid of the useless "stuff" that complicates your life and makes it less enjoyable.

How appropriate that I'd wind up talking to the brilliant George Carlin about "stuff" of sorts. It was a newspaper interview I was doing, and he told me about a pivotal point in his career. He'd been a very successful comic – but he had lost himself. His act was filled with "stuff" like The Hippy Dippy Weatherman, and the DJ from Wonderful WINO, an Indian Drill Sergeant, and Christopher Columbus' First Mate. He had written all these bits, great bits, and all these characters – but he wasn't in his act anymore. The "stuff" had taken over. He felt strangely uncomfortable. Lost. It wasn't till he dumped the "stuff" that he found "himself" – his core, his thoughts, his values, his ideas.

Now, "stuff" is great. There's all kinds of stuff. Fun stuff, memory stuff, helpful stuff, old stuff, new stuff, other people's stuff – it's great! Find it, keep it, trade it with your friends.

The problem only comes when the "stuff" starts to take over. When, instead of owning it, it owns you. When, instead of enjoying it, you require it. When you begin to define yourself by it. When you lose yourself in "stuff."

There's nothing wrong with "stuff." There is something wrong with losing yourself.

But, if you're worried you've lost yourself, there's good news!

Just look under your "stuff" – you're still there!

BILLY CRYSTAL

"Hugs"

"I went to the library, got out a book called HOW TO HUG – It turned out to be Volume 12 of The Encyclopedia Britannica."

— Billy Crystal as Buddy Young, Jr.

I remember being in the Green Room at NBC, 30 Rock, waiting for a taping of Tom Snyder's *The Tomorrow Show*. With me were Gene Siskel and Roger Ebert. I thought, "What a great gig they have, being paid to review movies."

Well, years later, I guess because I'm a comedian, a newspaper sent me to review the Billy Crystal movie *Mr. Saturday Night*. I wasn't thrilled with the assignment. (I'm not a big fan of *Pagliacci* – the pain behind the laughter, the tears behind the smile. What would they show me here? The anger of Mickey Rooney in *The Comedian*, the defeatism of Red Skelton in *The Clown*, the desperation of James Coco in *The Wild Party*, the self-servingness of Dick Van Dyke in *The Comic*, the arrogance of Jack Carter in *The Funny Farm*? Would it be a combination *Mickey One* (from the movie of the same name), Hecky Brown from *The Front*, Joe E. Lewis from *The Joker Is Wild*, with a little Willie Loman from *Death of a Salesman* and Mountain Rivera from *Requiem for a Heavyweight* thrown in for good measure?)

I walked in thinking I'd hate the film – and I walked out loving it. I knew I'd see the film again. I knew when it came out on video, I'd buy it. And when I reviewed it, I gave it high praise, not only because it was the definitive film about a journeyman comic (more realistic than *Punchline*, less lighthearted than *Always Leave 'Em Laughing*), but because Billy Crystal had put in a subplot, which in reading other reviews, I found that only I saw!

Certainly it's the story of a patchwork comic. You take Gene Baylos' hair, Jackie Gayle's eyes, George Burns' hands, Alan King's shoulders, Milton Berle's cigar, Henny Youngman's lips, Red Buttons' stance and almost everybody's material – and you've got Buddy Young, Jr. But even though he was put together with pieces of other people, he's not Frankenstein's monster, or, despite his flaws, any other kind of monster for that matter. Certainly it's a film about a sometimes angry, sometimes bitter man. Certainly it's a film about vanity, pressure, insecurity – and a mere mortal dealing with some human flaws caught in the spotlight.

But there's more here – a very interesting subplot.

What this really is, is a film about "Hugs."

Buddy's wife, Elaine, says it first – that he needs all the extra "hugs" that only an audience can give him. Buddy says it better himself, when in a comic eulogy to his mother, he remembers that the best place in the world was in her arms – more "hugs." Even Buddy's posture on stage, with arms outstretched, is a man asking for "hugs." And he shows it in the final scenes, when, in reconciling with his brother and his daughter, he does it by way of "hugs."

Let's talk about "hugs" for a minute. Hugs are important. There's a whole science called hug therapy.

Doctors admit that the body actually produces beneficial healing chemicals as a reaction to a warm, friendly hug.

"Backward" cultures with little or no modern-day medical advances produce healthier infants, simply because mothers constantly carry their babies in backpacks (thus giving them a body to hug), than do "highly advanced" cultures where babies spend most of their day in a crib or stroller.

Rabbits in a lab show no sign of high cholesterol even when fed high-cholesterol foods – if, when fed, they are petted, cuddled and hugged.

Something to this hugging thing! Why don't we do it more often?

I turned on the TV and there was my answer. Tom Snyder, now years later on CNBC, was complaining that people need to touch, but they've become so guarded, they're afraid to. In a mock comic tone he said – if you hug a female friend, they think you're having an affair – if you hug a kid, they think you're a pedophile. Such paranoia. He said, almost in a pleading tone, that he wasn't promoting lasciviousness when he talked about hugging; he was promoting friendship, compassion, warmth and caring.

I always did like Tom Snyder.

Personally, I have a feeling that the reason hugging is so quickly identified with "sex" is that, in our culture, everything is quickly identified with "sex." Why? Madison Avenue knows that "sex sells," so everything becomes linked with sex. Movies are "sex," song lyrics are "sex," books are "sex," toothpaste is "sex," deodorant is "sex," jeans are "sex," shampoo is "sex," and on, and on.

Well, folks, there are things other than sex, such as friendship, compassion, warmth, caring and hugs. Hugs don't have to be sexual. (When Madison Avenue figures out how to sell stuff with hugs, they'll put them in the forefront. Till then, for our own good, we'll have to do it ourselves!)

Hugs aren't sex – hugs are touching. And touching is important. Whether it's E.T. touching fingers with a little boy, or God touching fingers with Adam on the ceiling of the Sistine Chapel, touching is important.

Then I flipped the dial after the Snyder show and saw a bunch of lawyers hugging. They had just gone through intense sensitivity training. And each agreed that in learning how to be better people, they had become better, more effective lawyers. Something to this hugging stuff. Hug one another – it's good for you!

Saw a great bumper sticker – *Hugs, not Drugs!*

Football players hug after a touchdown. Classmates hug at a reunion. Families hug at a funeral. I saw co-workers hug at Cape Canaveral after a lift-off. Friends hug at airports. Survivors hug when they've been rescued. Political workers hug when they win an election. And everybody hugs on New Year's!

So what do you do if it's not New Year's, you don't play football, you don't live near the airport, or any of that other stuff? Here's a solution: Get a 24-hour-a-day, ready at a moment's notice hug partner – get a pet!

(Don't get me wrong – hug as many people as you can, but for those extra hugs, get a pet!) Pets love hugs. They beg for them, they purr for them! Dogs can't get enough. There's a line in the Broadway show *Cats* – "Touch me and you will know what happiness is!"

My wife, Suzanne, twisted my arm till we got pets. I was against it. You see, I was allergic. And I didn't need anyone else to hug. God had given me the greatest "hug" partner in the world, my wife. Suzanne's the kind of person you want to hug ten minutes after you know her. She's the most caring, empathic person in the world. I always said if my wife and Mother Theresa got to the Pearly Gates at the same time, St. Peter would let my wife in first! (Hey, she has to be a saint – she puts up with me!) It's no wonder that she's helped so many patients, children and adults, in her psychology practice (I saw her take one child who hadn't spoken in two years and turn her into a little chatterbox). The kids call her "Dr. Suzy" (Watch out, Dr. Phil!). So she persevered till we found pets that didn't make me sneeze. I literally auditioned them; five minutes each, on my lap in a closed room, till we found the sneeze-proof ones. Best move I could have made.

Studies show that just hugging a pet can give you a longer and healthier life!

So look into getting a pet. And to make it even more special, get your pet from the SPCA. That's where my wife and I got our collie "Sable" and our Persian "Fluffy." You'll be saving your pet's life – and it may be saving yours!

And if you live in an apartment and can't get a pet, I have one more suggestion, contribute to comedian Elayne Boosler's "pet" charity, Tails of Joy, which saves abused pets, and finds them loving homes with lots of hugs.

But whether it's pets or humans, give (and get) all the hugs you can!

Because as Buddy Young, Jr. says, "What we need is love today!"

MINNIE, MICKEY, AND UNCLE DIRTY

On Love

"So, some of us country girls went to the Christmas Dance, just a-lookin' for love. It was so much fun! I didn't do any dancin'. I didn't want anyone to steal my spot – under the mistletoe!

"So we kinda had this contest to see who would get kissed the most that night. The plan was the next morning we would meet, and we'd compare notes. Now, being lady-like and all, we had this code word. When we met the next day, every time we said the word 'morning,' it stood for one time we were kissed.

"So my one friend came out and said, 'Good morning this morning' (she got kissed twice).

"My next friend said, 'Good morning this morning, what a beautiful morning it is this morning!'

"My third friend said, 'Good morning this morning, what a beautiful morning it is this morning. I love morning. Morning is my favorite part of the day. I just love morning, morning, morning!'

"And I just said, 'Howdy!'"

– Minnie Pearl

Everyone is looking for love. Comedians maybe most of all. And Cousin Minnie Pearl is one of the most beloved comedians of all time. I mean, how many comedians had a museum built for them? More should. Well, if you'd gone to Opryland (as in Grand Ole) in Nashville, TN, that's exactly what you would have seen – the Minnie Pearl Museum.

I met this legendary lady once after a show. What a joy!

She told me a great story about the first time she ever went out on that big stage. She was nervous, worried. Thoughts of "What if they don't like me? What if they don't like my jokes?" started to prey on her. And then a fellow performer gave her this advice – "Just love 'em – and they'll love ya back!" She did, and the rest is history!

What a great thought: Just love 'em – and they'll love ya back!

And it's true – they will. But that doesn't say they'll all love ya back!

Now, we'd all like everyone to love us, but not all people love the same thing. Any cracker-barrel philosopher will tell you – that's why they make chocolate and vanilla and strawberry, too! Vanilla doesn't sit around and worry that not everybody loves it. You just can't get everyone to love you.

Maybe comedians know that best of all. Take jokes. Any comedian will tell you that you can do the same jokes for 100 nights, and 99 nights the crowds will love 'em. And on the other night – as Joan Rivers said, "Oh, well!"

Let's talk about that other night. I was booked at The Tabas Resort Hotel where I had played twice before and done very well. (So I got return engagements.) But on this third night – oh, well. No use getting into why, it was just – oh, well! As if I didn't feel badly enough (I was only in the business about a year, still wet behind the ears), to add insult to injury, when the bar manager paid me he said, "Spend it wisely!" The inference was "you won't be returning."

As I walked through the lobby taking it pretty hard, there, checking in, was Mickey Rooney. My photo was in the lobby, so he looked at me and said, "Were you the comic tonight?" I said, "Yes" and hoped he wouldn't pursue it. But he did. "How did it go?" Mixed in with a dozen compliments of having just seen him in *Sugar Babies* – I told him my tale of woe.

"Well, son, don't take it too hard – you must be good, they brought you back twice! Hey, they can't all love ya. Heck, I've been married seven times – I'm living proof of that! But you've gotta keep trying. If every baby quit every time he fell, none of us would have ever learned to walk."

"You love it, don't you, kid?" he said. "I can see it in your face. You just keep doing what you love! Go out there every night and have a ball – give it everything you've got!"

I told him it looked like I might not be back. He said, "Don't worry! Who knows, your next job might be right around the corner – or right across the street!" He wished me luck, I thanked him over and over for the kind words, and he left.

I walked into the parking lot, and looked across the highway at the other big resort hotel in town. The Downingtown Inn. I knew it well. It was my real college. You see during my college years I was there every night I could. Beverage manager Scottie Howden would wave the drink minimum (in that I was under age) and let me in to watch great comics like Dick Shawn, Marty Allen, Jack Carter, Jan Murray, Soupy Sales, Jackie Mason, Marty Brill, Phil Jaye, Fisher and Marks, Joe Mauro, Sal Richards, Jack Wakefield, Ralph Pope, Joey Villa, Mickey Manners, Don Sebastian, Curtis & Tracy, Gannon & Gerstenblatt, Jay Jason, Gene Brenner, Bobby Shields, Dick Lord, Bobby Gold, Bob Melvin, Jack Eagle, Bobby Ramsen, Dave Kent, Tom Patterson, Mark Russell, Irwin C. Watson, Lenny Rush, Greg Lewis, Gus Christie, so many more. Could I work there? What the heck, it was worth a try. And it was "right across the street!"

I walked in and introduced myself around. The next thing you know, thanks to entertainment director Merle Besecker, I was in the general manager's office. Luckily, he had seen me across the street on one of the good nights. He had liked what he saw (I never figured out if in his mind I was vanilla, chocolate or strawberry, but I didn't care; all I knew was, he liked it!). So I got an audition, and from it I got 13 weeks of work.

I was back doing what I loved – and taking my chances nightly!

I learned to love it no matter what, unconditionally. Not thinking about a desired result, or an expected result, or a deserved result. I was back to loving just doing it. Eventually I was back at the first hotel, too – once word got out that I was a success at the second. Thanks again, Mickey.

There is such joy in the act of loving unconditionally without expecting anything in return!

Some people love stamp collecting – the stamps don't love them back. Some people love a good book – the book doesn't love them back. Granted, loving people is more complex; riskier, but take that chance. Love people, love things – love life!

Just the thrill of loving is its own reward. (Say, a 50% reward.)

If you are loved back – that's even more of a reward. (Say, the other 50%.)

As they say, "Half a loaf is better than none!"

Now, you can never guarantee 100% -- but you can guarantee 50% every time – just by loving!

Once, I was asked to do a radio interview with Uncle Dirty (Bob Altman), a great comic who came from the days of coffee houses, where you could be as much a philosopher as a funnyman – and he is both. At the end of an hour interview, philosophizing about everything from politics to peace and love and the good old human condition, he left me with a thought that pretty well sums it up:

> "In life, not to be loved – is miserable.
> But not to love – is a catastrophe!"

BILLY GLASON

And the First List of Ten

*"Ad in the Classifieds: FOR SALE – Complete Encyclopedia
Set – Never been used -- My kids know everything!"*

– from *Billy Glason's Funmaster Gag Files*

While most of the funny people in this book need no introduction
in that they are, or were at one time, household names – Billy Glason is a
bit different. Billy was a household name, but only to people in the world
of comedy.

In the early '70s, when I learned at Billy's knee, he'd say, "You smart
alecks think you know everything – listen and learn!" Long before *Star
Wars,* I knew what it was like to meet Yoda. Billy was Yoda. When it came
to comedy – Billy knew.

Billy was an old vaudevillian. I mean old. He was so old, he wouldn't
tell you his age. He called George Burns "Junior." Billy lived around the
corner from the Stage Deli in New York, where you could get a sandwich
named after Shecky Greene or Danny Thomas. In his prime, he had
traveled the country more than 50 times over. He was one of the best
singer/comics in vaudeville. Never a "big-name attraction," just a solid,
reliable laugh-getter. In his own words, "The big stars would bring 'em
in – then guys like us would entertain 'em!"

But the road was behind him now. He was in his apartment. Probably
hadn't been out of it in 10 years. He had invitations all over his desk:
Red Buttons – "Come see me!" Milton Berle – "Come visit." The Friars –

"Come to lunch." *The American Comedy Awards* – "Be our guest for the ceremonies!" He wouldn't go. He was comfortable in his home. Comfortable with his reputation. Comfortable. Billy was The Comedy Doctor. He could fix any act! Diagnose the problem. Dispense the right advice.

The big stars always mentioned him in interviews – Johnny Carson, Flip Wilson, everyone. He had carved a very special niche for himself. He had, in his years of vaudeville, amassed a trunk full of jokes, which he turned into a joke file. Jokes on every topic. They were old, but tried and true. And every major comedian at one time or another, whether they would admit to it or not, used his services. Comedians subscribed to his newsletters. Comedy writers bought his joke files. Speakers and disc jockeys bought his volumes of *Classified Gags*. And would-be emcees bought his books on *How to Master the Ceremonies*. The big stars bought his $3,000.00 *Comedy Encyclopedia*. (I used every saved dollar from 18 years of birthdays, Christmases, graduations, and tooth fairy visits to buy one, too.)

To those who were really devoted, willing to travel to the mountain top, Billy would personally teach all the tricks of the trade – joke construction, routining, delivery, etc., in a stream-of-consciousness lecture that had gold in every word. If you could write fast enough, you could catch it all. But it would take years to fully understand.

Among all my other notes, I found these particularly interesting bits of advice:

> #1 *Focus on one goal.* Don't let anything dilute it!
> (Billy said focus on one important thing – being funny. Don't let other things distract you. Don't be distracted by money, or glory, or glamour, or glitter. Focus on your goal. Be determined, and you will reach it!)
>
> #2 *Don't idolize anyone so much that you lose yourself!*
> (It was okay to learn from Gleason, or Skelton, or Carson or Carlin, but don't ever copy them, because then that's all you'll be: a copy. You'll lose yourself and be a second-rate Carson instead of a first-rate you! The world has a first-rate Carson. It needs a first-rate You!)

#3 *Work hard, but give yourself a day off!*
(Billy said, "Comedy – 7 days a week – gets very unfunny!"
When it starts to get tedious and stops making you laugh,
take a break. We all need a day of rest.)

#4 *Don't use profanity!*
(Billy admitted profanity was good for a "shock laugh,"
but it would never get you an invitation to a network
TV show, or a White House gala, or a Royal command
performance. Have class. Have dignity – even if you wear
baggy pants!)

#5 *Don't ever perform in a place you wouldn't invite your
father or mother to!*
(Billy called 'em "cockroach joints." The kind of places best
kept off résumés. The kind of places you didn't talk about
in mixed company. Your time is better spent rehearsing
for the better-class venues. You'll get to them, if you don't
waste your time and talents in the other places.)

#6 *Don't ever steal somebody's original material!*
(There are plenty of "stock jokes" in joke books to pick
from. Use them, re-word them; they are public domain.
Fit them to your style. Don't steal another person's act or
style. Be different! Ten people can tell the same joke in ten
different ways. Find your own way!)

#7 *Don't lie when you tell a joke!*
(If you were never "poor," don't do jokes like "I was so
poor that..." If you were never "fat," don't do jokes like "I
was so fat that..." Don't do them because they won't ring
true. Always be honest – that will be funny! Then you
will succeed!)

#8 *Don't envy another comedian's success!*
(Envy can destroy you. It can eat away at you. It can
make you throw away all the things you've worked for in
a foolish attempt to get what somebody else has. You don't
need what somebody else has. You won't enjoy it. You only

need what you deserve. You'll get it if you persevere. And when you get it, boy will you enjoy it!)

#9 *Don't try to kill another act!*
(Don't walk onstage wanting to one-up the act before you or outshine the act after you. Don't walk onstage looking to destroy. That's negative. Go onstage trying to be your best. That's positive. That will succeed!)

#10 *Let your act be pure, unadulterated you!*
(Entertain, inform, amuse, do whatever is you, but stick to it. Don't weaken the act by going outside it for something extra that isn't you. That will only dilute it and make it less honest, less you. Once you find what rings true for you, stay with it and you'll succeed).

Those are 10 pretty good pieces of advice!

It took me awhile to realize that these bits of advice, if you changed the wording and order a little, were written in stone a few thousand years ago on a couple of tablets!

> *And as God said when He gave the tablets to Moses – "Take two and see Me in the morning!"*
>
> also from *Billy Glason's Funmaster Gagfile*

DICK GREGORY AND DANNY THOMAS
and a Hopeful Prayer

"The Supreme Court can't really be effective in getting prayer out of the schools. After all, what else can a kid do when it's exam time and he hasn't studied all semester?"

– Dick Gregory

It's funny how different generations see the same person in a different light. In the '80s, younger people might have seen Dick Gregory as a health-food expert. In the '70s, my generation saw him as a civil rights leader and activist. In the very early '60s, he was seen as a brilliant nightclub comic in the era of Lenny Bruce and Mort Sahl. I've been around long enough to have seen him as all three. But I thought of him primarily as a thinking man. A person with a deep understanding of humanity. A man to be respected.

So when I saw him standing on the corner of 3rd and Chestnut Streets in Philadelphia one day, I yelled to my driving buddy, comedian John Briggs, "Stop the car!" (It's the only time I've ever yelled "Stop the car!" in my life. Everyone should do it just once. It's a great rush.)

I got an even bigger rush seeing Dick Gregory. The only reason I was downtown was to go to an afternoon sound check at a nightclub where I was performing that evening. As I approached Dick Gregory with my friend John, I just started to gush – "Dick Gregory... you're terrific... I saw you at The Main Point in 1977... I'm performing at a club right around the corner tonight... blah blah blah... blah blah blah."

I was like a little kid who had seen Mickey Mantle. Not only was this man a major comic with TV, record and concert credits as long as your arm, but he was there in the trenches on the serious side with John Kennedy and Martin Luther King. He was a significant part of history. And he was talking to me. Wow!

We spoke for awhile about comedy, and changes, and life. When we parted, he left me with a phrase that still rings in my ears. As he extended his hand to say good-bye, he said, "Keep me in your prayers."

"Keep me in your prayers?" Wow. Not what I expected. Not from someone who came through the last three decades as they were.

From someone who had seen the assassinations and the bigotry upfront, the Watergates and politics as usual, I expected something more humanistic, more cynical, more hardened.

This was a man who above all saw through the bull----. He did it in his comedy, he did it in his writing, he did it in his philosophy. But, "Keep me in your prayers?" That gave me something to think about.

It had been a long time since I had thought about "prayers."

The first time I ever truly thought about prayers (not just recited them but really thought about them) came from the words of another comedian, Danny Thomas. (Yep, not from a priest, or a nun, or a rabbi – but a comedian.)

I was five years old and (as journalist Steven Rea wrote in a feature story in *The Philadelphia Inquirer*) I was the only kid in my first-grade class allowed to stay up till 9 o'clock to watch *The Danny Thomas Show*. Of course, now four year olds watch *David Letterman*! But this was a different era. I had worked a deal with my parents that as long as I got straight A's, I could stay up late and watch Danny Thomas on TV. (It was my job then to act out the whole show the next day on the playground for my deprived classmates.)

Well, one week Danny Thomas told a very real and heartrending story about a time in his career when he was married, broke, with a family, no job, and at a crossroads. He went into a church and prayed to St. Jude (the patron saint of hopeless causes). He simply asked, "Let me find my way and I will build you a shrine," wanting more than anything to be a success in show business. He claims an inner voice came to him saying over and over, "Go to Chicago." He listened to it, became Chicago's toast of the town and launched a career that in 20 years made him a major star in show business. (To this day, in Memphis, TN, there stands The St. Jude Hospital for Children, treating children with catastrophic diseases, regardless of a family's ability to pay. It was built, through much fund-raising, as a memorial to an answered prayer.)

Well, after the Dick Gregory comment, I thought about prayer, and Danny Thomas' story kept reeling in my head.

Interesting that Danny Thomas prayed to the patron of the hopeless. It got me to thinking, maybe that's what prayer is all about – hope.

How many times have you heard the statement – He hasn't got a prayer! It's synonymous with – There is no hope!

But, interestingly, as long as he's got a prayer – there's hope!

As long as we can pray, we can hang on to one last thread of hope – and so long as we can hope – all is not lost!

Dick Gregory had seen it all: hatred, assassination, lying, corruption – but he still said, "Keep me in your prayers!" (i.e., "Keep praying" – "Keep the hope" – and "Keep me a part of that hope"). Wow.

Sometimes things all come together.

As I was laying in a hospital bed (after Chapter One) avoiding some thoughts and bandaged almost from head to toe, I heard from a visiting comic, Norm Klar, that a local nightclub owner was putting out the word that I'd never walk onstage again.

I said a prayer, "Please let me keep being able to do this – all I ever wanted to do was make people laugh." Three days later I was released from the hospital, still in heavy bandages and casts. Two days after that I was scheduled to do a previously booked show at La Salle University.

I had never missed a show in my life, and I wasn't about to miss this one.

I knew I couldn't stay on stage for 40 minutes – I could barely stand. So I booked some comedians around me to fill the time (one being Norm Klar, who literally carried me house-to-car-to-stage). I had them introduce me as "Direct from The Fitzgerald-Mercy Hospital Emergency Room – Tommy Moore." I went out in casts and bandages, did doctor jokes, hospital jokes, operating room jokes – and got laughs!

When it was all over, some of the kids in the audience came back to "schmooze" and were amazed that my bandages and casts were real. They thought it was a gimmick just made up for the act. That's when I realized my prayer had been answered!

That's when I also recalled that, just before I walked on stage, I said to the comics, "Say a prayer for me out there!"

Always keep the hope.

There's a great story about W. C. Fields (long a drinker and carouser), who, toward the end of his life, sat on a hospital bed staring at an open Bible. A friend came in, and never knowing Fields to be a religious man, he said, "What are you doing?" To which Fields answered – "Looking for loopholes!"

Always keep the hope.

JACKIE VERNON

Cooperation vs. Competition

"My grandfather used to say 'Happiness is like potato salad -- spread it around, and you've got a picnic!'"

"I tried to lose weight. For a year I ate nothing but dehydrated foods: dehydrated meats, dehydrated fruit, dehydrated vegetables; then one day I drank a glass of water – gained a hundred pounds!"

"I'm never lucky. Once, I opened a fortune cookie – I found a summons!"

– Jackie Vernon

The rotund Jackie Vernon (well known as the voice of *Frosty the Snowman*) had a comic reputation of being the dull guy, a chronic loser, a corpulent oaf. That was his nightclub act anyway. In real life, he was anything but dull. Sitting with most people for hours in an airport can be, by definition, boring. But not with Jackie. He had stories of the road that were fascinating: stories of playing small clubs, stories of playing rough clubs, stories of playing strip clubs (most of which can't be repeated in mixed company). When I booked him for our comedy club, as our first big-name headliner, I guess I heard them all. In the three days we spent together, I hung on every word. But the stories I remember most were the ones about the camaraderie that existed among comics when Jackie was a youngster in the business.

He told me stories of the Catskills and Calumet City, where, after the shows, comics would gather, hang out, usually at all-night diners, and pool their resources. In those days, comics did two or three shows a night to audiences that didn't always change. So the jokes had better change, show to show. That's where the "pool" came in.

Comics would come "to the table" with all the new jokes they'd heard and dole them out appropriately. If you were fat, and somebody had a "fat joke" – he gave it to you. If another comic was bald, and you had a "bald joke" – you gave it to him. Poor jokes, wife jokes, loser jokes, whatever – by the time you left "the table," you were armed with enough ammunition to last you all week.

He said the young comics who ran our comedy club seemed to be like that somewhat, at least in a helpful spirit. And for quite some time, we were.

It was a comedy club owned, operated and staffed by comedians. The ticket-taker was a comedian, the sound man was a comedian, the ushers were comedians – "One for all and all for one." It was a great place, kind of like *The Little Rascals* clubhouse.

One day, in a scene right out of the movie *Punchline*, we decided to have a comedy competition. The "pro" comics (i.e., those who had at least a year or two's seniority) were out of the running. This was to benefit the younger comics; to give them some stage time, some recognition, and a shot at an appearance on local TV (that was the grand prize). Everyone was excited about it. Well, it seemed to be a good idea at the time. It wasn't.

People looked forward to that night for weeks. But from the minute the night began, something was wrong. Something was in the air. The spirit of serious competition was pervasive.

This wasn't a just-for-fun softball game or a pie-eating contest. This was real competition. Every one of the twenty comedians involved was unusually quiet, unfriendly. Each found his or her own little corner. Each jockeyed for position in the show. Each rehearsed his or her lines with less of the excitement of giving a performance and more of the worry of winning. There was a definite feeling of tension, even in the audience. With each act, we felt we were seeing less fun and more desperation. Worse yet, little psyche-out games were being played backstage, comments designed to undermine the confidence of fellow comics. The feeling was definitely – "there's only one prize, and I've got to win it. I've got to be better than you." No one backstage seemed happy to be there. And no one seemed proud of their feelings.

Then it happened. A desperate move. A comedian on stage (who I will leave un-named), did two jokes directly from the act of a female comic who was to follow. These weren't "stock jokes," mind you; these weren't "public domain." These were jokes written by, original to, and very crucial in the act to follow. Her name was Susan Shulman. I saw her face drop when it happened. Her whole act had been weakened. Two of her best jokes had just been taken. She was shaken.

I immediately went to her husband and asked, "Do you mind if I talk to her?" She was quietly "stressing out" near the ladies' room. I went over to her and pinned her to the wall. I literally shouted in her face, "FORGET WHAT JUST HAPPENED. JOKES DON'T MATTER. YOU ARE FUNNY. THAT'S WHAT MATTERS. NOW FORGET THE JOKES. GO OUT THERE AND BE FUNNY!" There was no time for her to think about it. Just as I finished my "pep talk," they called her name. Susan took the stage – and without her best jokes, won the contest. She later thanked me. She deserved to win. She was talented and hard working. (Years later I would see her on an episode of *Seinfeld* – it was nice to see.)

Everyone was glad Susan won. But no one left that night feeling good. No one left feeling friendly. No one left feeling anything had been accomplished. There were 19 losers and one winner. The competition had brought out some emotions that no one was proud of. It was the first and last competition we ever had.

But there was another night. What a night!

A very funny lady named Abby Stein had been seriously ill. Big hospital bills. And even though she was a New York comic, she had a lot of friends at our Philly comedy club. We decided to do a fund raiser for her.

Everyone pitched in. Some did publicity, some sold tickets. I went on *AM Philadelphia*, and with the help of hosts Janet Davies and Dave Roberts, told all of Philadelphia to come out. Every comic in Philly donated time. Everybody in town appeared for free. There was even a carload of New York comics who drove down to help out. There was Will Miller, Jim Tam, Lou DiMaggio, Jim Myers, and the not-yet-famous Rosie O'Donnell. And no one pulled rank, no one jockeyed for position.

From the moment comics started showing up, it was like a family reunion. Hugging, backslapping – and talk about cooperation! Acts were discussing material at the bar so that no two covered the same topics. Everyone was out to make this the best, most coordinated show possible.

Almost 40 comedians took the stage for five minutes each, and the audience was as good for the last as it was for the first. They saw a spectacular show, with a display of camaraderie that was a joy. Comics were high-fiving each other as they walked on and off the stage. The crowd tore the roof off the place. And by the time the evening was over, we raised a few thousand dollars, got a few thousand laughs, and left feeling good.

That night we all learned something –

Cooperation is so much better than competition.
It accomplishes so much more.
Fosters the best in people.
And makes everyone a winner!

We had all brought something to Jackie Vernon's proverbial "table" and walked away so much richer.

It's not unusual that so many of my thoughts of Jackie Vernon involve food. It seemed we were always at a restaurant, or a hoagie joint, or in a supermarket shopping for some snacks for "later." Jackie loved a good meal, so it's appropriate that when I think of him, I think of this story. It's not a joke. It's an old fable I heard one weary a.m. on one of those spiritual moments TV had before they signed off for the night. As I said, it's not a joke, but it certainly has a strong punch line!

A guy dies. He goes to a place, he knows not where.

An angel meets him and takes him to a room.

They open the door, and there before them is a grand banquet hall: a mile-long table with posh chairs, the finest silverware, and the most elaborate cuisine ever displayed.

"This must be heaven," said the man.

"No!" said the angel, "This is hell!"

And with that, a dinner bell rang. Two doors opened and in came hordes of skinny, scrawny, emaciated people. They just sat at the table and cursed.

"Why don't they eat?" asked the man.

"Because their elbows don't bend," replied the angel. "And when they try to feed themselves, they can't. So they just sit, gnash their teeth and curse their fate. And that's the hell of it!"

Then the angel took the man to a second room. They opened the door, and here was the exact same banquet hall: same chairs, same silverware, same cuisine. But this time when the dinner bell rang and the doors opened, in came throngs of fat, happy people, joking and laughing as they entered.

"This is heaven," said the angel.

"I see," said the man. "In heaven their elbows bend."

"No," said the angel, "In heaven their elbows don't bend, either. But when these people realized they couldn't feed themselves, they reached across the table and fed each other!"

That's the best definition of heaven and hell I've ever heard.

Maybe it can be heaven on earth, if we're willing to give up the selfishness.

"Life is a banquet – and most poor fools are starving to death!"

– from the Broadway play, *MAME*

"A joyful spirit is at a continuous banquet."

from the BIBLE (Proverbs 15:15)

SAM LEVENSON

Teach!

"I had a student once who said, 'I ain't got no pencils'...I told him, it's: I don't have any pencils, you don't have any pencils, he, she, or it doesn't have any pencils, we don't have any pencils, you don't have any pencils, they don't have any pencils.
He said, 'Who's got all the pencils?'"

— Sam Levenson

Sam Levenson was maybe the first American comedian to come from a teaching background. (Others to follow would be Bill Cosby, Robert Klein, Dennis Wolfberg and Joy Behar).

All living things are teachers of sorts, at least by example. When we teach, we leave tracks in the road for others to follow. If we teach good things, we leave, as country comedian and singer Kenny Price used to say, "Happy tracks". And if we leave happy tracks, when the day is done we can look in the mirror and be happy with what we see. My father taught me that.

It was November 9th, 1968 (I remember the date 'cause I still have the flier). I was a teenager in an audience of people three times my age. Sam Levenson was my favorite comedian of the day. And here, at The Cherry Hill Jewish Community Center, pencil and paper in hand, I was taking notes at his lecture/comedy show.

Mr. Levenson said something very shocking to me. He said, "We are teaching kids all the wrong things. We're teaching them facts, but not humanity. And so we are turning out educated brutes that act like barbarians!" Yes, the world had spun around a few times since the days of teachers who taught character first, subjects second.

A few years later, doing my student teaching in pursuit of my B.S. in Elementary Ed. (which was only to please my parents – I knew all I ever wanted to be was a comedian), I realized that if I could handle a room full of 5th graders for five hours a day, handling a nightclub full of patrons for an hour a night would be a breeze.

Well, this one day, the students decided to be… well, barbarians. It was time to ad lib. I took the big green metal army issue trash can (remember those?) and dropped it on the floor. CLANG! Then I took each book and as I dropped them in the trash can I said, "Arithmetic – *Garbage*… History – *Garbage* … Geography – *Garbage*… None of it means anything if you don't learn how to be decent people first! Today we're going to learn to be decent people." I won't talk about the bullying that ignited my surprise lecture, but let's just say I taught an impromptu lesson on "Do unto Others!"

I've always thought that Sam Levenson was right. What we're taught becomes what we learn. What we learn becomes what we think. What we think becomes what we believe. What we believe becomes what we do. And what we do becomes who we are.

If a child isn't taught Greek – don't expect him to speak Greek! And to fully have a language learned it must be learned, required, and used, at home, in the community, in the media, and in the workplace 24/7. To have it become part of a person's character, the person must learn it, speak it, write it, and even think in that language. The same goes for ethics.

If the child isn't taught kindness, compassion, understanding, and respect (for themselves and others) – don't expect it to be part of their character later in life. I always thought that maybe we should get the Amish to redesign the curriculum.

When, 30 years later, I would hear Ellen DeGeneres say, "We should teach Compassion in school. We should teach it every day, as a subject, like Arithmetic and History, Compassion and Kindness," I thought, "Bravo."

Kindness. When newspaper reporter Beth D'Adonno reviewed my act as a "kinder, gentler brand of comedy" (from the XXX-rated stuff that had become comedy club fare) I started thinking about kindness.

Mark Twain said, "Kindness is the language that the deaf can hear and the blind can see." (The first time I ever saw that phrase was on Buddy Hackett's tour jacket.)

Ron Gaylord, of the comedy team Gaylord & Holiday, wrote a melody to the words of Steven Grellet's poem, "I will pass this way but once, if there's any good thing I can do, let me do it now."

Comedians are some of the kindest, most giving people ever. Danny Thomas said, at a St. Jude Benefit, "Entertainers take the only thing they have to sell...and give it away." We all know of the biggest charities: Danny Thomas with St. Jude Hospital (with the torch now in the good hands of his daughter, Marlo), Jerry Lewis with MDA, Danny Kaye with UNICEF, Whoopi Goldberg, Billy Crystal, Robin Williams, and everyone with Comic Relief. But the list of comedians who have helped raise money for other charities would fill a book by itself. We've all done countless charities.

Comedian Al Costante, emceeing a charity benefit, used the catch phrase he uses after every joke (like Rodney's "No Respect"). Al's catch phrase, in response to the laughter was, "You're too kind!" As I waited to go on with impressionist Will Neri (who probably did every benefit there was, too) I thought, especially this night, how much kindness there was out there.

Sometimes we get knocked around and our hearts get hardened and our souls begin to die. But the greatest way to get our heart and soul back is to start doing little (or big) acts of kindness. As Bert Lahr once said, "Always give a piece of sugar to a horse."

In the late '80s, comedian Robbie Roman (one of the kindest, gentlest souls I ever met) was asked a favor by a booker who had a reputation for abusing people. Robbie said, "Yes, I'll do that for you," and with a look that would stop a charging army, he added, "but don't ever mistake my kindness for weakness."

Kindness isn't weakness. Kindness is great strength. Sam Levenson taught, "Do you want some strength building exercises? Bend over to help a child. Reach out to help an old person. Lift someone's spirits."

Yes, doing those things will make others happy, and you happier when you look in the mirror. But teaching them (if only by example) will leave a legacy. It will leave happy tracks.

Teach.

COZY, MICKEY, MY UNCLE, DAD, AND MOM
For Everything, a Time

"I love those little old ladies who go to funerals with one thing on their minds—'Where's my flowers?'"

—Cozy Morley

"So this fella's been drinking all night. In his condition, anything looks like anything. He wanders into a funeral. Instead of kneeling at the coffin, he kneels down at the piano. When he gets up, he says, 'The guy in the box doesn't look so good, but he's got a great set of teeth!'"

–Mickey Shaughnessy

Cozy Morley and Mickey Shaughnessy were two of the comedy superstars of Wildwood N.J., and as a kid, going 'down the shore' didn't mean 'the beach' to me, it meant going to see each of them at their respective clubs.

Cozy put on a three-hour variety show at his Club Avalon, with the likes of comedians Julie DeJohn, Tony Santoro, Fisher and Marks, and Hayden and Rodgers; singers like Don Cherry, Carmel Quinn, and The Winged Victory Chorus; novelty acts like magician Jimmy Ray and the dance team Kikks; and superstars like Joey Bishop, Johnny Ray, and Dennis Day, who he would vary each summer to make it a whole new show every year. But what stayed the same was Cozy. He'd do a half hour of jokes up front, emcee the show, and then close with another hour plus of comedy and music, playing five instruments and doing sing-a-longs to his signature songs like *He Was All Dolled Up* and *On the Way to Cape May*. His act was like a party, and his audience was like a group of neighbors, family, and friends at a yearly reunion.

Mickey held forth at his Club Lou Booth. The night would open with The Joan Rodgers Trio, and then Mickey would take over. He could weave stories into jokes, do an Army induction routine wearing an Army-issue pea coat and boots, and then transition into growing up in an Irish neighborhood (and make you forget he was still in Army gear!) His career took him to character parts in dozens of Hollywood movies like *From Here to Eternity* and Elvis Presley's *Jailhouse Rock*, but every summer, he was right back in Wildwood.

Twenty-five years later, in my adult years, they would both help my career — Mickey by getting me jobs at places like The Villas Boat Club, and Cozy by doing a New York Times interview with me and saying, in print, "You're terrific, kid. You take over for me when I'm gone." What a thrill!

But in every August of my youth, each of these masters would make me laugh, and for a while I'd forget the impending sadness and despair that was but a few short weeks away – school!

Funny how, for a while, (despite my youthful distaste for academia), I became a teacher. And when I taught my course in *Humor as a Life Skill* at Temple University, I always taught that laughter could wash away the clouds of sadness and despair. It came from all those comedians – and from having a funny family that never let sadness last too long.

The scene was a very somber one: my mother's Cousin Jimmy's funeral. My Uncle Schnazz was a very funny man. He was later banned from funerals because he made people laugh so hard they couldn't mourn. Well, there's Jimmy, lying in the box. Jimmy had been a life-long gambler. He would gamble on anything. If two raindrops were sliding down a window pane, Jimmy would bet on which one got to the bottom first.

In walks Uncle Schnazz. "Hold it, everybody," he says. "Hold it." He has the room's attention. Uncle Schnazz goes over to the coffin, taps on the side and says, "Jimmy, there's a crap game in the alley!" He waits a second, looks up, turns to the crowd and says, "Yep, he's dead!" Everybody laughed.

I always remember laughter in our house, and laughter has pulled me out of many emotional ruts, some even more devastating than that little incident in chapter one.

Every week, for years, my father took me down to the record store to buy me a new comedy album. I played them on my record player like some kids played The Beatles, over and over. I still remember the first five I picked out: Myron Cohen, Pat Cooper, Pigmeat Markham, Bill Cosby, and Redd Foxx, probably spanning the gamut of comedy styles. (Today I have one of the biggest comedy LP collections in the country.) There was always laughter in our house on the record player, on the TV, or at the kitchen table.

My dad told stories every night at the table. Laughter was as much a part of dinner as the food. My dad had been an assistant manager at several vaudeville theaters in his youth, and he told me stories of the greats of that era. Now he was a shipbuilder, and he had a way of turning everyday occurrences into stories, sometimes to whisk away sorrow.

One day he came home early, having been burned on the arm and leg during an accident at the shipyard. I was worried. Here's the story he told: "So I go to the dispensary and the doctor asks me to roll up both sleeves. I told him that I only burned my right arm. He said he wanted to compare the two. Then he told me to roll up both pant legs. I told him I'd only burned my right leg. He said he wanted to compare the two...When he was done I said, 'It's a good thing I didn't burn anything else, Doc – I've only got one of them!'" He said it made all the nurses laugh. More importantly, he made me laugh, and my worries about his injury were gone in an instant. If he could laugh about it, he must be okay!

I loved my father. I could tell you a hundred stories about the kind of man he was, but I'd rather tell about the kind of boy he was. My uncle told me that at age 12, right in the heart of the Depression, my father would take his little red wagon down to the food distribution warehouses, find the food that was in broken crates or cartons (and therefore couldn't be sold), and load up his red wagon, bringing it home to distribute to the whole neighborhood. If that's the kind of kid he was, you can imagine the kind of man he became.

I was proud of my father. And I also got the enormous thrill of learning that he was proud of me. Once, when I was half asleep in the other room, I heard him tell my aunt the reason he bought me all those albums was that he was so proud of me fighting to keep my grades up.

(I have to give Mom a story here. I was 12 years old and in a book store with my mother. I picked up a book called *The Essential Lenny Bruce*. It had some pretty racy stuff in it, but it was about a comedian, so I wanted it. When I went to the counter, the clerk refused to sell it to me. I told my mom. She took a few minutes and paged through the book. She went to the clerk and said, "This is my son. Sell him the book." Go Mom!)

I was a good student, a persistent student, but I hated to read. I had some problems to fight. They didn't have names in those days like ADD or dyslexia. They were just called, "You have to concentrate more!" I learned how to concentrate. Sometimes I concentrated too much, especially on devastating events. We all have those.

As an adult, nothing hit me harder than my father's death. I was ruined. And then one day, my father's voice came to me and said, "That's enough!" So I did a strange thing. I asked my wife Suzanne to go to Wildwood, New Jersey, with me to see two great nightclub comedians, Cozy Morley and Mickey Shaughnessy.

As a kid, at my begging, my father had taken me to see both of them every year, at their respective nightclubs, where each had become a legend. (Since kids aren't normally allowed in nightclubs, my father did whatever it took to get me in.)

Now, as an adult mourning my father, I was seeing these great comics again.

Cozy Morley did a piece, banjo in hand, about how the tone of a New Orleans' funeral turned jubilant after the proper time of solemnity, with a parade down Bourbon Street.

The next night, Mickey Shaughnessy told all the funny stories of what happened after an Irish wake at the "party" that followed. And I laughed.

There needs to be a time of rejoicing after the sadness of death. Those of us who believe in heaven have a reason. We can see our loved ones in "a better place." It's at least one good reason to believe in heaven. But everyone can rejoice in the good times they shared with their friend or relative while he or she was on earth. I've been to some ceremonies where the friends and family were asked to come to the microphone and do just that – share the happy, funny stories about their loved one. It's a wonderful experience to "rejoice" – to "re-evoke joy" in the world.

I can only say from personal experience that first you must go through the anger and the sorrow. But one time through them is enough for anyone. Anger revisited just re-opens old wounds. Holding onto sorrow keeps them open. Only laughter and good thoughts can start the healing. And that is what your loved one would want for you.

I knew that laughter always worked for me; I was sure it would work for others. And I was given the proof when the following story happened:

I was standing in the rear of my own comedy club one night waiting to go on, surveying everything. (When you have your own club, you learn to survey everything all the time). I noticed a commotion in the back row. A customer got up and left the building. I went over to his friend and asked if anything was wrong. He told me that the man who had left was having some emotional troubles. I left it at that. The opening comedian went on, then the next, and during that act I saw the second man get up, as well, now leaving their two wives wondering.

In about 30 minutes, I heard my introduction. I went on stage, and from the corner of my eye, I saw the two men return and take their seats. What was going on? Would there be trouble? I didn't know. I was on guard. As I did my act, I kept them in view. The second man was laughing immediately, so I knew he was no problem. But the first man had a scowl. What was going on? Little by little I saw his mood brighten. In 10 minutes he was laughing; by 15, I knew everything was going to be all right. And it was.

After the show, as people came to say hello, the first man, now all smiles, came and said, "Thank you for making me laugh." And as he left, the second man, his friend, doubled back and said, "I've got to tell you what happened. When my friend left, I had an idea where he'd be going. That's why I went to find him. He had left the club and walked a few blocks in the cold to the Vietnam War Vets Memorial. I found him there, sitting against the wall, in the cold and drizzle. He told me he just wanted to be with his buddies. I told him I understood, but that we should be getting back to our wives. He came back, and you made him laugh. I want to thank you for my buddy."

I said, "He already thanked me – but thank you for letting me know why!"

People sometimes question "making light" in a sad situation. But I know that "making light" can "lighten the burden."

BOBBY COLLINS

E-liminate the Negative!

"Had a bad day. Just flew back from Mexico. 'El Cheapo' Airlines. It was great. If they don't guess your weight – you get on free! I got nervous when I saw them strap my luggage to the roof. Then I ate the food. A taco. I love Mexican food. Your body makes noises you've never heard it make! It's like you have a mariachi band inside you! Oh well, we all have bad days – you just have to wrap up your underwear, mail it home in a manila envelope – and keep trying!"

– Bobby Collins

"YOU'VE GOTTA FORGET ALL THAT NEGATIVE STUFF – AND JUST WORK FROM YOUR HEART!" roared Bobby Collins, long before he was the star of VH1's *Comedy Spotlight.*

That statement takes about 5 seconds to deliver. That doesn't sound like a lot of time, but when you've only got 3 minutes to be as funny as you can, every second counts. To spend 5 whole seconds on something serious takes guts!

Let me explain:

The producers of *People Are Talking*, a Philadelphia TV talk show then hosted by Maury Povich, called and asked me for some advice. I had done their show a few times, so they considered me something of a comedy expert. They needed a comedian who could be as funny as humanly possible in just 3 minutes. (Not an easy task – it takes some comics 2 minutes just to say hello!) I told them there was only one answer – my friend, Bobby Collins. They said they wanted to see him. I replied – "You don't have to see him, just book him, introduce him, and relax!" They had faith in my judgment.

Bobby arrived. We rehearsed the bit, for time, in the green room. Three minutes on the dot. And amidst a barrage of physical, facial, verbal and observational humor was that statement – "You've got to forget all the negative stuff and just work from your heart!" It was the one calming force in a piece that was otherwise a frenetic whirlwind of explosive scattershot comedy. It was, in fact, a life statement, the backbone of the piece. Bobby's positive humor scored big!

Later, at lunch, I asked how he remained so positive on stage when some of our peers in comedy-club-land were so cynical, cutting, caustic, downright negative and mean-spirited in their humor. I just wanted to see what he'd say. "You oughta know that," he said, "you're a clown, just like me. You're circus folk! We're not up there to depress them. Why would anyone want to do that? We're up there to make 'em happy. So you've gotta fight those negative thoughts!" I knew that's what he'd say – I just wanted to hear him say it!

I once heard that Liza Minnelli visited the bedside of singer-dancer Ben Vereen after his almost fatal accident. She forced him to join her in a duet of "You've got to Accentuate the Positive, E-liminate the Negative!" So, trying to keep that in mind, I promised back in Chapter One to answer a few questions – well, here goes:

How did I get out of my little predicament I was tied up in back there?

Sheer determination that my wife wouldn't come home to find a dead husband lying on the floor, or worse, a live mugger lying in wait, made me fight my way out of the situation! (The sight of my wife's face at the hospital was like an angelic vision.)

Some not-so-misspent hours in a magic store as a kid reading Houdini books gave me the knowledge to work my way out of the ropes around my neck, hands, and feet! (I later called the magicians who ran the shop – Marty Martin and Larry Taylor – to thank them.)

Some heightened powers of awareness got me to slip back into the ropes when I heard Mr. Mugger returning to check on me, and then slip out of them again when I thought he had left.

A power from somewhere higher gave my broken fingers and arms the ability to unlock and push open doors. (I thanked that Power later, too!)

And the kind of guts my father gave me, the kind it takes to walk on stage, not knowing who's gonna be on the other side of the curtain when it opens, gave me the drive to open that final door, not knowing if Mr. Mugger would be waiting for me there. (I said a prayer that he wouldn't be. He wasn't.)

Thanks to neighbors and passing motorists who made phone calls when they saw my bloody figure struggling down the street, and to some great EMS people, I got to the ER of Fitzgerald-Mercy Hospital.

Thanks to some great surgeons, I was put together as good as new, like the Scarecrow in the repair shop at Oz. (I kept telling them, "While you're working on those 186 stitches in my head, put in some hair plugs – I'm a little thin on top!") They didn't, but God bless them for what they did.

Thanks to the police and a 24-hour guard on my hospital door, I felt safe. You see, the police honestly believed that Mr. Mugger, still on the loose, might come to the hospital to finish the job. They knew something I didn't.

And thanks to great detective work, and reward money donated by a friend, Mr. Mugger was caught. He got life plus 52 years. I went to court a lot to see to that. It seems they needed me. I was just one of the folks he had mugged. I was, unfortunately, the only one who lived. I guess I ended a crime streak.

(As for Mr. Mugger, I wish him no malice. In fact, I hope he can buy lottery tickets in jail, and I hope he hits the lottery for at least 1.5 million dollars. You see, I've been awarded a civil judgment against him for 1.5 million dollars. Don't think I'll ever see that though).

Since then, I've realized that we all meet many thieves in our lives:

Some are people. Some are places. Some are things.
Some will try to steal your joy
Others will try to destroy your dream.
Some will try to take your very life.
But they are all the same.
Learn to deal with one – and you can deal with them all!

So that's the story. And through it all, amid all the negativity, even at the moments I thought I was going to die, the one good picture that kept popping up in my mind was of audiences filled with laughing people. That's what was in my heart. So I took Bobby's advice, pushed the negative stuff out of my head and worked from my heart, getting back to doing what I really wanted to do – make people laugh.

From that day when they told me I might never get on a stage again, I've been on stage thousands of times. Some have been in comedy clubs, resort hotels, corporate boardrooms, college campuses, on TV, even in hospitals. Some have been doing seminars, lectures, keynote speeches or just plain shows.

But through all the variables, one thing has remained the same: I've always ended my show with the same bit of advice.

Once, after my 300th show at Caesars, someone asked me, for probably the 50th time, to write it down. And so I did, in longhand, in my dressing room, then handed it to him with an autograph.

It's what I say at the end of every show:

> *Tonight we've had some music,*
> *and some magic,*
> *and some laughs.*
> *If you remember nothing else from my show, please remember this:*
> *There's more music in the fact that the waves lap against the shore than in all the songs ever written!*

*There's more magic in the fact that the stars light up the sky
than in all the tricks ever invented!
And there's more laughter in the funny, silly things we do
every day than in all the jokes ever told!*

*Learn to listen for the music,
Learn to look for the magic,
Learn to hear the laughter,
and every day,
you'll have a ticket
to the greatest show on earth,
YOUR LIFE!
God Bless You.*

GEORGE BURNS

And One More Thing

"I promise to tell the truth, the whole truth, and nothing but the truth, so help me – Me!"

– George Burns, from the movie *Oh, God!*

Why am I devoting another chapter to George Burns? Well, if you live to be a hundred, I'll give you two chapters, too!

Besides, it's just a little chapter. And it comes with a warning. Don't read on unless you are religious – or curious.

OK. Back a few chapters, when I asked Mr. Burns for some advice on being in show business, aside from the joke about the wallet in the dressing room, he later told me one more thing – "Always get to know the theater manager – talk to the manager – and get on his or her good side!"

You see, a theater manager can do a lot for you. He or she can overlook some mistakes, forgive others, smooth out the rough spots, run interference, provide help when needed, and generally make life easier. And just knowing that the manager's on your side gives you a sense of power and comfort.

Now, George Burns spent the last part of his career in a unique pursuit. Playing God in three great movies. By all means rent them. But it's a strange thing about God – everybody's got a different name for God. Some call God – The Prime Mover, or – The Force. A hundred different religions have a hundred different names for God. Pianist Roger Miller had a sign in his dressing room that read – "Luck is God's nickname!"

I like to call God – The Manager.

And then remember Mr. Burns' advice:

"Always get to know The Manager – talk to The Manager – and get on His or Her good side!"

JERRY CLOWER

"Ain't God Good!"

"I'm convinced that there's just one place where there is no laughter – that's in hell…and I have made plans not to go there!"

– Jerry Clower

Up till now I've talked about the advice comedians have given me for happiness in *this* life. But how about after this life? How about the afterlife?

Well, country comic Jerry Clower taught me a thing or two about that.

Jerry was affectionately known as "The Mouth of the South."

I love the South.

I did my first ever show, at age 20, in a church in the South. (Yes, I was a clean enough comic to work in a church). It was The Trinity Lutheran Church, at 18th and Wolf, in South *Philadelphia*. Yep, I was born and raised up North.

South Philly. It was a truly warm place. A place where people knew each other, and watched out for each other. It was a true melting pot of America. The sights and sounds and foods and customs of the old world were there. And with them, a lot of love. People visited each other unannounced. And when they visited they brought food, ricotta pie, cream-filled cannolis, or baked ziti. There would be hugging and back slapping. And I heard the phrase, "God Bless You," a lot.

And the first time I visited relatives South of The Mason Dixon Line, in Laurinburg, North Carolina, I felt the same warmth and love. People visited each other unannounced. Only here, with the hugging and the back slapping, there was pecan pie, Little Debbie Cookies, and pork barbeque. And I thankfully heard the phrase "God Bless You" a lot, too.

As I picked up the local paper, I was excited to see that Jerry Clower was appearing at a church in Fayetteville. Problem was, the paper was three days old, and the concert had come and gone. But I picked up a Jerry Clower record album at a Piggly Wiggly grocery store in North Carolina (they don't sell comedy albums in grocery stores up North), and I soon was hooked on Jerry Clower's warm storytelling ways. Good thing, too – 'cause 15 years later when I was invited to portray Jerry Clower in a review called *Honky Tonk Angels*, I didn't need any rehearsals!

Jerry always talked about God, especially in his video, *Ain't God Good*, (which I thoroughly recommend!), and in this chapter I'll be talking a lot about God, too. I say that as a warning, 'cause whenever you talk about God, politics, or Amway, people get nervous. They think you're trying to sell them something. I'm not. I'm presenting this in a strictly biographical context. I believe deeply in God and Heaven. Whether you do is, and should be, solely up to you.

People don't usually associate God and Heaven with laughter, even though Psalm 2:4 says, "He who sits in Heaven laughs!" Maybe you didn't know that. I didn't, till I was directed to it by Jerry.

The church I went to often focused on sorrow, and pain, and misery.

Garrison Keillor once said something like, "We come from a stock that believes life is full of misery and sorrow, and if anything good does happen, you should wait, and it will pass."

Sorrow. One night in Wildwood, New Jersey, I was feeling really sorry for myself. I showed up for 3 nights of shows, to find the restaurant dark and locked up. I called the owner, contract in hand, saying, "What's going on? I'm supposed to be here Monday, Tuesday, and Wednesday!" He said, "No, it's Tuesday and Wednesday."

Not by my contract, but there had been a mistake. So here I was, stranded, not getting paid for the night, and feeling sorry for myself. Well, the owner got me a motel room, and my friend Baxter, who had driven me down, stayed with me for a couple of hours to cheer me up, but I was still pretty miserable. With nothing better to do, I turned on the motel's TV. The first things on the screen were words from the Bible, "In the world you will have tribulation – but be of good cheer, for I have overcome the world!" It was the Resurrection scene from the 1927 silent film version of *King of Kings*. And H.B. Warner, portraying Jesus, had just said those words.

"Be of good cheer" I thought? Jesus said that? I never heard that before. "Be of good cheer, for I have overcome the world." Cheerfulness was not something they talked about a lot where I went to church – solemnity, seriousness, graveness yes, but not cheerfulness. I guess they weren't thinking beyond the 'grave'.

In the next few months, via people like Jerry Savelle, Gordon Douglas, Joyce Meyer, Charles Swindoll, Jesse Duplantis, Joel Osteen, Roy Hicks, Kathryn Kuhlman, Albert Cliffe, John Hagee, and Creflo Dollar, comedian Joey Adams' book *The God Bit*, and the Website *God's Yellow Pages*, I got directed to other quotes from the Bible:

"I come to bring you Joy!"

"The Joy of the Lord is our strength."

"The Joy of the Lord, no man can take from you."

"This is the day the Lord hath made – let us Rejoice and be Glad!"

"Count it all Joy."

How could this be, talking of joy, with all the misery in the world? I had forgotten the second part of the quote, "In the world you will have tribulations, but be of good cheer, for I have overcome the world!"

Overcoming. We've done some of that. My friend, and fellow comedian Baxter, got me to admit that the only time I've ever cried onstage was at the finale of a show I was in called *Gospel Train*, for three wonderful people – Marilyn, Will, and Carrie Roy of Ace in The Hole Productions, in North Jersey. It had only been a short while since 9/11, and the country was still reeling. So when The Chain of Love Quartet had us all hold hands, cast and crew, audience and wait staff, young and old, black and white, and sing *We Shall Overcome*, it had a special meaning.

Sometimes it feels overwhelming, like everything in the world has gone wrong! And it's at those times that you most need to hold onto your joy and be of good cheer. Because the Bible says, "A merry heart doeth good!"... I'd like to philosophically add that a heart filled with anger, frustration, hatred, jealousy, or fear is more likely to do bad. (That's from personal experience!)

But how can you keep a "Merry Heart" when everything in this world looks rotten?

Well, just remember, this world isn't all there is!

As I was preparing to do a show once in a hotel in King of Prussia, PA, I wandered into the gift shop. There was a giant button that said, "Enjoy life – this isn't a dress rehearsal!" I bought it 'cause I thought it was cute. But the more I thought about it, the more I thought it should read, "Enjoy life – it's only a dress rehearsal!"

I say that because when everything in the world seems wrong (like when everything goes wrong in a dress rehearsal), we should work to overcome it, because there is something else, something after this world. There is a place, I believe, called Heaven.

And don't let the thieves tell you, "There ain't nothing else!" Don't let them steal your hope, or your faith, or by embittering you, steal your love as well. 'Cause love is essential. Let me repeat that, *Love is Essential!* Because, to paraphrase the Bible, if you have a lot of stuff, but you don't have love – you don't have anything.

The Beatles said, "All you need is Love!"

Somebody said, "God is Love."
So it logically follows, "All we need is God!"

Jesus said, "Love God... Love one another...Do unto others as you would have them do unto you... Forgive and you shall be forgiven... Judge not and you will not be judged...Give and you shall receive...Fear not... Believe...and Be of Good Cheer!" That's kind of the Cliff's Notes version to staying on the right path in the "Directions to Heaven." It's a GPS of sorts. God's Positioning System.

(By the way, I know there are those who don't believe in Heaven. I do, though. And to you others, I can only say that if everyone followed those instructions above, it'd be more like Heaven right here on Earth!)

Now, when it comes to Heaven, I know that who gets in is not my call. It's God's.

And as the Bible says, although it is hard for a rich man to get through Heaven's gates, "What is not possible with man is possible with God." So the next time you think your neighbor won't get in, next time you think you may not get in...don't fear, don't judge ... just try "getting in good" with God. He's The Manager. It's His call.

My favorite religious joke goes like this:

A man dies, goes to Heaven. St Peter meets him and says, "Before you get into the main room, there's a full-day orientation. What faith were you?" The man tells him, and St Peter directs him to the proper orientation room. "If you get lost, you'll see the name of each faith on the door. There's Baptist, Catholic, Lutheran, Jewish, Episcopalian, Buddhist, Methodist, Muslim, Greek Orthodox, there are about 2,000 doors. And as you go by each one, please don't make any noise." The man says, "Why not?" St Peter says, "'Cause they all think they're the only ones here!"

God can let anyone in He wants, even a Samaritan; even a Publican, even a Prodigal Son, even a worker who slept till noon.

So make it your "job" to "get in good" with God. As Jerry Clower used to say, "As jobs go, the benefits are GREAT and the RETIREMENT PACKAGE can't be beat!"

Now, why do I believe there is a God? Well, it's not because anyone told me, or because I read it in a book. I'm cynical enough to doubt that. Nope, it's because I have too much firsthand experience. I can't even count the number of times when I was in big trouble, the kind I couldn't handle, and I said, "God, I put this in your hands!" And immediately, and I do mean immediately, the problem was gone. And I'm talking every kind of problem: health, social, financial. Every time.

I'll tell you about one of those times. Maybe the most dramatic. I've kept it a secret till now. I was afraid people would think differently about me if they knew. But here goes.

It was a financially bad time in my career. You know, starving comedian. I was two thousand dollars behind on the house, and the bank was threatening to foreclose. I knew two things – I had $20 in my pocket and $40 in the bank. (When you're really broke, you know exactly how much money you have, and where it is.) I also knew I had $250 coming in that week, and that wasn't enough.

I went to church, got down on my knees and said, "God, I need $2,000.00 from somewhere. And at this point, it has to be from You." And I prayed. When the collection plate came around, I put all I had in, the $20. After all, $20 wasn't going to help me that much. So I gave it to the Lord.

Now, at the time, I didn't know anything about The Widow's Mite, or the 100 Fold, but I did know I had to tap the local ATM for part of my last $40 bucks. And so I did. I took out ten dollars. I don't know why I looked at the balance. I knew what it would be. But I was wrong. The balance was $2,030.

How could this be? Was there a misprint? Had God given me two thousand? I knew I had to go to the bank the next morning. If there was a mistake, I didn't want any of the clerks getting in trouble.

9:00 a.m. I was at the bank. (I was a nightclub comedian – I very seldom saw 9:00 a.m.) But there I was, the bank's first customer. I explained the situation to the bank president. He looked into it and found the error. He thanked me for my honesty and deducted it from my account.

I went home feeling good; that I had done the right thing, but a little queasy, knowing that I needed that $2,000. I turned on the TV. It was, by chance, on a religious program. The first words I heard were, "If God wants you to have something, you will have it."

Three days later I got a letter from the bank, with a statement showing the deduction. A day after that, I had sparingly used up the $10, so I went to the bank for ten more. My balance – was $2,020!

I went to the bank president again, and a bit flabbergasted, I explained that the two thousand was still there.

"I know," he said, "I can't figure it out!" He said that every day for the past week, he had deducted the $2,000, and the next day, when he checked, it was always back in!

"At this point," he said, "it's screwing up our bookwork. I'm going to let it be!"

The words rang in my ears all the way home, "When God wants you to have something, you will have it."

That speaks to me!

I kept the story a secret for years. Why tell it now?

Well, one day, coming back from Laurinburg, North Carolina, I heard Elvis on the radio. He was singing an old spiritual, and the lyrics went:

"It is no secret what God can do.
What He's done for others, He'll do for you."

Please remember, I am cynical. I'm in show business; I've been lied to a lot. You've got to prove something to me before I believe it.

Also, I'm a performer. Ask any performer why they do things a certain way, and the most basic answer they will give you is – Because It Works!

God works. And if you want more than my firsthand knowledge, read a book called *The God Bit* by comedian Joey Adams.

God works.

That is my belief.

As Jerry Clower would say, "Aint God Good!"

STEVE HARVEY
The Best Advice

So you've read this book, and you're saying to yourself, "Tommy, after all this advice you've gotten, you must be the happiest, most peaceful guy ever." Nope. I get aggravated, frustrated, overwhelmed, and impatient. Why? Because I get too busy, too distracted, too intimidated by society to even *remember* some of this advice – much less follow it! (That's why I have to re-read my own book every once in a while.)

But let me tell you a story of one time when I was really overwhelmed. Went to bed thinking, "What's the use?" Couldn't get a restful sleep, and the next thing you know it was morning, 7:24 by the clock. I was used to waking up to Adult Contemporary music. (It's really soothing to wake up to Nat King Cole, Steve Lawrence, Sammy Davis Jr., Frank Sinatra, Count Basie). But somehow the dial had been switched to what seemed to be a black evangelist preacher. The first words I heard were, "When things seem overwhelming, put God in your life... This is Steve Harvey."

Wow! That shocked me. Steve Harvey? The comedian? From *The Steve Harvey Show* and *The Kings of Comedy* tour? Yes, he now had a radio show. That really made an impression on me. As I lingered in bed, mulling over what he had said, in a way I would not if it had come from someone else, my wife, Suzanne, who had gone downstairs to make breakfast, yelled up to me, "Go back to sleep – it's not 7:30 – it's 6:30."

Every clock in the house said 6:30, except our bedroom alarm – that said 7:30.

What happened here?

Well, somehow, our alarm showed the WRONG time.

The radio dial had moved to the WRONG station.

And it went off precisely in time to give me the RIGHT message… delivered by the RIGHT messenger.

Steve Harvey said, "When things seem overwhelming, Put God in Your Life!"

Talk about a Wake-Up Call!

I think of all the advice in this book, that's probably the best!

Thank you, Steve.

And thank you, God.

AFTERWORD

I've seen this prayer written many different ways, in many different places. It has been prayed by clowns as diverse as Red Skelton and Steven G. Brenner. It's been said that *Saturday Nigh Live* comedian Chris Farley carried an abbreviated version in his wallet. Since it has always been credited as anonymous, as I do now, it's impossible to determine which version is the original, but this is the one I like best:

A CLOWN'S PRAYER

Dear Lord:
Help me to cause more smiles than frowns,
Create more laughter than tears,
Scatter more sunshine than rain,
Dispense more happiness than gloom,
Spread more cheer than despair.

Never let me know fame or fortune to the extent that I will forget or
neglect my friends.
Never let me become so indifferent that I will fail to see the wonder in
the eyes of a child, or the twinkle in the eyes of the aged.

Never let me forget that my total effort is to cheer people,
make them happy, and make them forget, at least momentarily,
all the unpleasantness in their lives.

Never let me attain financial success to the point
that I will stop calling upon my Creator in my hour of need,
or thanking Him in my hour of plenty.

I am thankful for the million non-accidental miles I have traveled,
the million people I have entertained,
and the million laughs I have had.

Please help me to ease the strain of life for people of all ages,
to demonstrate the kindness that links all hearts,
and to bring joy wherever I perform.

Protect all clowns, watch over us, and forgive our mistakes.
Help us to give our best performance always.
Let us all be present in the back yard of heaven when the whistle blows.

And in my final moment,
May I hear you whisper,
"When you made my people smile, you made Me smile."

In Jesus' name. AMEN

Comedian Tommy Moore is a man of many hats – all of them funny.

As a performer, he's headlined over 350 times at Caesars Resort Hotels, hundreds of Comedy Clubs, Cruise Ships, Casinos, Colleges, and Country Clubs, and appeared over 100 times on TV and Radio, as well as opening for people like Bobby Rydell, Dionne Warwick, Chubby Checker, The Coasters, The Platters, Jay Black & The Americans, Loretta Lynn, Janie Frickie and many more.

As a newspaper columnist, in his *Comedy Corner* column of 12 years, he's reviewed or interviewed just about every comedian in the country.

As a teacher, he's taught at Philadelphia's Temple University, where he got the title "Professor of FUN™," with courses like *Stand-up Comedy Performance, Humor as a Life Skill, The History of American Comedy, The Legends of Comedy,* and *Comedians – from A to Z.*

As a writer, he's contributed to *Mad Magazine, Reader's Digest, Parade Magazine,* and *The Official Joke Books.*

As a broadcaster, for 3 years of feature segments on *The Out on The Town TV Show,* he's gotten his head chopped off, learned belly dancing, tried sword swallowing, and was generally "up for anything."

As a lecturer, he's presented his *Laugh Away the Stress* programs at corporations like AT&T, DuPont, American Express, Sony, and hundreds more.

As a Comedy Club owner-producer, he's hired everybody from Rosie O'Donnell to Soupy Sales and rubbed elbows with everyone from Steve Allen to George Burns.

He's recorded 3 CD's, *The Great American Joke Book, Jokes You Can Tell in Church,* and *Jokes I Heard on The Golf Course...* with more to follow.

His act is a combination of jokes, stories, one-liners, hats, props, audience participation, stunts, magic tricks (that usually don't work), and sometimes even a sing-a-long. His mission statement is to "Use humor to Entertain, Inform, Uplift, and Heal." And he's proudest of the fact that, doing a clean act, he's been able to perform at venues as varied as Churches, Synagogues, Senior Centers, and The USO.

This is his first book. Learn more about him at www.profcomedy.com.

Printed in the United States
By Bookmasters